a Palladian Villa in Bristol

Clifton Hill House and the People who lived there

Annie Burnside

redcliffe

To my husband, Marc, and my sons, Olivier and Philip

First published in 2009 by Redcliffe Press Ltd.
81g Pembroke Road, Bristol BS8 3EA
T: 0117 973 7207
E: info@redcliffepress.co.uk
www.redcliffepress.co.uk

© Annie Burnside (text) and Stephen Morris (selected photographs)
ISBN 978 - 1 - 906593 - 34 - 6
British Library Cataloguing-in-Publication Data
A catalogue record for this book is available from the British Library

Design, new interior photography and layout Stephen Morris www.stephen-morris.co.uk
Printed by HSW, Tonypandy, Rhondda

Contents

Foreword

As the year of the centenary of Clifton Hill House as a hall of residence approached, I thought it would be a good idea to write a history of the house from the time of its construction to the present day. Students and staff I talked to were enthusiastic; they wanted to know more about their Hall. With the help and enthusiasm of many people – some acknowledged on page 136 – this book is the result.

Annie Burnside

A Palladian Villa

Clifton Hill House was built between 1746 and 1750 as a most imposing semi-rural villa of Palladian inspiration for Paul Fisher, a highly successful linen draper, very wealthy merchant and ship-owner. At the height of his wealth, Fisher employed Isaac Ware, the Palladian architect and designer of national renown and protégé of Lord Burlington. During his Italian 'Grand Tour' in the early 1700s, Lord Burlington, the aristocrat and gifted architect, was inspired by the neo-classical designs of the sixteenth-century Italian architects, Giulio Romano and Andrea Palladio. Burlington visited Rome with its temples, and Vicenza where Palladio built numerous 'neo-classical country retreats' for wealthy Venetians.

On his return from Italy, Burlington's ideas soon gained currency, giving rise to a 'dictatorship of taste' that made it 'de rigueur' to emulate the architecture of the Ancients. Burlington was pleased to give his patronage to young artists and architects such as Colen Campbell, William Kent and Isaac Ware. In 1727, Burlington designed Chiswick House which became an inspiration for Clifton Hill House, as was Marble Hill built by Colen Campbell between 1724 and 1729.

Fisher chose Clifton as the site for his villa, following the growing fashion for building in suburbs far removed from the dirty, bustling and industrial parts of the city:

> The city lived within an acrid cloud of smoke thrown out from glass works, brass foundries, sugar refineries, ironworks and suburban collieries. For more than half of each day retreating tides exposed stinking mud banks, where ships lay on their sides like so many drunken aldermen.[1]

Alexander Pope was just as categorical:

> The City of Bristol itself is very unpleasant, and no civilised Company in it…The streets are as crowded as London,…tis as if Wapping and Southwark were ten-times as big.[2]

Even some thirty years later the city of Bristol was still most insalubrious; Horace

Chiswick House built by Lord Burlington in 1727.

Marble Hill, built by Colen Campbell 1724/1729.

Portrait of Isaac Ware and his daughter by the Italian artist, Andrea Soldi.[4]
Isaac Ware is pointing proudly at the plans of Wrotham Park in Middlesex.

Frontispiece of Isaac Ware's translation of Palladio's *I Quattro Libri* dedicated to Lord Burlington in 1738.

Walpole in a letter to his friend Lord Montague declared:

> I did go to Bristol, the dirtiest great shop I ever saw, with so foul a river, that, had I seen the least appearance of cleanliness, I should have concluded they washed all their linen in it, as they do at Paris.[3]

Fisher bought the land on Clifton Hill stretching down to Clifton Wood and the river. The views were impressive, even more so than today, as Bellevue had not yet been built.

Clifton Hill House was Ware's first work in the villa style. He designed two more in Scotland, and in 1754, he built Wrotham Park in Middlesex for Admiral Byng. His designs for both Wrotham Park and Clifton Hill House feature in his treatise on architecture of 1756, *A Complete Body of Architecture*.

In 1738, Ware dedicated his translation of Palladio's famous treatise on architecture *I Quattro Libri dell'Architettura* to Lord Burlington, and by the time he designed Clifton Hill House, Ware was a practising architect of national repute, and also Clerk of Works to King George II. He is regarded as the architect responsible for the second revival of Palladianism in England.

The exterior

The construction of Clifton Hill House was to be that 'of a country seat without columns, or other expensive decorations.'[5]

The house is a simple astylar 1-3-1 villa with a tall central block flanked by low service wings. It is built of local pennant grit faced with Bath stone for the main façades. The restrained, but highly competent, design must have suited Fisher's earnest and unpretentious temperament:

> His family is moderate; he intends to build for convenience more than magnificence, but he will have the house handsome though not pompous.[6]

The carvings in the tympanum of the west and east pediments are the only ornaments on the two façades. The east front of the house overlooks the sloping gardens; unusually and because of the fall of the ground, the rustication comes up to the 'piano nobile'. The basement is of heavy vermiculated masonry and there is smooth stonework for the upper floors. The piano nobile is of hewn stonework which contrasts both with the vermiculated rustication of the podium and the smooth ashlar of the top two floors.

The overwhelming impression is of height and the main block must have seemed even taller before the Victorian addition of flanking single-storey wings in 1853 and 1890. There are three floors above the level of the basement which is finished with a wide platband from which the piano nobile rises. The central three bays are set forward only slightly. 'The forefront of the house is to project a little forwarder than the two ends.'[7]

Above each window of the piano nobile are three voussoirs with the central keystone almost reaching the first floor platband. The windows of the upper two floors are simple squares and double squares without architraves, cut directly into the smooth ashlar of the façade.

The only decorative element of the garden front elevation, apart from the Italianate staircase, is the cartouche carved with Fisher's arms. The cartouche rests between floral festoons and pendants and occupies the crowning pediment of the house. Though Professor Mowl speaks of 'the chilly serenity of Isaac Ware's designs',[8] the fine carving of rococo inspiration lessens the Palladian austerity of the façade; Fisher's armorial shield featuring three fish is probably a rebus connected to his name. The gracious dove, the highly decorative flowers and leaves of the festoons that seem to hold the armorial shield are the work of Thomas Paty, the famous Bristol mason and carver. His name appears in the house accounts as one of the most highly paid craftsmen. He received over £2,000 for his work at Clifton Hill House between 1746 and 1750. His name is also linked with many more buildings in Bristol, and in particular with the Royal Fort (1758/1761).

The imposing and elegant Italianate flight of steps with turned balusters was greatly inspired by Burlington's staircase at Chiswick House. It has a heavily rusticated double perron with vermiculated stonework to match the rest of the podium; it leads from the piano nobile onto the garden terrace. Ware, in his treatise *A Complete Body of Architecture*, says:

> The flight of steps also is a very great ornament to the edifice… and when the basement storey is faced with rustic, it gives an air of solidity to the superstructure, it looks as a

Garden side: plate 40 from Isaac Ware's *A Complete Body of Architecture*, 1756.

Garden side with the added nineteenth-century wings.

Fisher's armorial shield is held between floral festoons and pendants. The carving is by Thomas Paty.

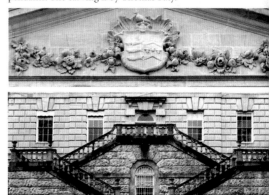

The Italianate staircase with vermiculated rustication.

The 1853 south wing.

The north wing with the Victorian balcony.

Gibbs surround and rustic stone blocks.

rock upon which all the rest is raised.[9]

The vermiculated rustication is rendered by tooling the stone to imitate the tufa (volcanic stone) found in the neighbourhood of Rome.

In 1853, Dr Symonds, the Bristol physician who bought Clifton Hill House in 1851, added the south wing. The basement storey was heightened, thus providing an extra reception room where Dr Symonds entertained the literary and artistic élite of his time. This addition is in keeping with Ware's elevation, though the tall windows of single panes clash with the more elegant Georgian windows of Ware's elevation. A fine balustrade surmounts the parapet with five decorative balls set at regular intervals.

The north wing was added in the 1890s, long after the Symonds family had left Clifton Hill House to settle definitively in Davos. From there, John Addington Symonds wrote:

I was so interested to hear about C.H. House. Is it not beautiful, that garden and that view! I wish I cd get a photo of the new front.[10]

The house was, at that time, tenanted by the prosperous Bristol brewer, William John Rogers. This new wing provided him and his family with another grand reception room. It also brought symmetry to the garden side elevation.

The stonework is identical on both wings but instead of the three modest window boxes of the 1853 wing, there is on the north wing a long and imposing balcony with heavy Victorian ironwork.

The west front

Originally, the west elevation was identical to the east façade with a 1/3/1/ bay design and hewn stone rustication. However, in the nineteenth century a screen wall and a porch were added for Dr Symonds. These alterations, though sympathetically done, mean that the two façades are no longer identical.

The new doorway with its heavy Gibbs surround and rustic blocks was designed to echo the east entrance door of the garden side.

Thomas Paty's finely carved monogram of Paul and Mary Fisher with the date

1747, adorns the tympanum of the pediment of the west elevation. The letters P M and F, are beautifully entwined and give a light relief to the severity of the façade.

Clifton Hill House influenced a number of buildings in Bristol, the Royal Fort House (1758/1762) in particular. In the latter part of the eighteenth century some buildings were even straight copies of Clifton Hill House on a reduced scale: Hartford House in Dighton Street near the Bristol Royal Infirmary (probably by Thomas Paty), and Mortimer House on Clifton Down. Mortimer House is a closer paraphrase of Clifton Hill House without the vermiculated rustication or the imposing Palladian staircase. Ware's designs for Clifton Hill House were copied further afield than in Bristol:

> The Irish were to build an exact copy of Clifton Hill House at Crosshaven in Co Cork eight years later, firm evidence of at least a one-way movement across the Irish Sea.[11]

The interior

The interior of the House is calculated to combine convenience and effect while omitting the sort of parade rooms found in the aristocratic villa, which would have been inappropriate to Fisher's life-style. The main rooms are disposed symmetrically on either side of a central axial corridor.

The Porch was added in the 1850s by Dr Symonds, it is in the shape of a cube and leads to the original corridor that extends through the house from the west entrance to the east entrance door that opens onto the perron on the garden side. It is divided into two sections, the west side being the finer of the two; it comprises three bays of cross vaulting enriched with fine plasterwork of chains of delicate bellflowers and bosses. The vault rises from scrolled consoles bearing acanthus leaves. The six-panelled doors are each surmounted by a pulvinated pediment.

The main stair hall is accessed to the right of the corridor. The background walls are fairly plain with classical motifs of egg-and-dart and Vitruvian scrolls.

The staircase itself (the first cantilevered stone staircase in Bristol) rises to two storeys with a blind balustrade below the window at the first floor level; it has fine and elaborately scrolled wrought-iron balusters with foliage sprays and fern-leaves. This fine and innovative ironwork inspired similar iron railings at the Royal Fort in the 1760s.

Monogram of Paul and Mary Fisher with the date 1747.

above:
Pre-1900 postcard of the west front showing the nineteenth-century screen wall and heavy Gibbs surround.

right:
the corridor extends the width of the house.

Clifton Hill House. Ground-story plan

Ground-storey plan, fig.22 of *A Complete Body of Architecture*. The plan appears in reverse but clearly shows the layout of the house.

The Porch was added in the 1850s.

right: Diana in the Fisher Drawing Room.

The ceiling is a typical Ware arrangement of oval and oblong panels, the central panel containing elaborate and fanciful rococo plasterwork. Joseph Thomas, the talented Bristol tiler and plasterer, indulged in a lively design of acanthus and 'C' scrolls and shells. There is an interesting tension between the rich motifs of the rococo style that Ware called 'the French ornament', and the geometrical austerity of the Palladian panels typical of Inigo Jones's ceilings. The four spandrels bear a shell with an acanthus scroll and small garlands. Joseph Thomas was paid £406 for his magnificent plasterwork in the house.

More rococo plasterwork is to be found in the two main reception rooms of the 'piano nobile'. The pulvinated pediments above the doors are also worth noting. They give a sense of proportion and some architectural importance to them. Samuel Glascodine was the house carpenter. His name also is connected with other buildings in Bristol.

The south-east Reception Room marked 'Drawing Room' on Ware's floor plan, is known today as the Fisher Drawing Room; it has an elaborate ceiling with delicate rocaille details contained within a formal Palladian arrangement of panels. The four spandrels of the ceiling have fine and lively rococo swirls and an elaborate cornice with the egg-and-dart and other classical motifs. The plaster decorations by Joseph Thomas are remarkable: in particular the delightful carvings of the heads of Ceres, Diana, Bacchante and of an unknown Goddess. Diana's head is adorned with her iconic crescent, her smiling face looks at her quiver and arrows; delicate cornucopias and elegant rococo scrolls in the shape of hound heads constitute a welcome relief from the severity of the geometrical Palladian compartments. Ceres's

head is adorned with ears of corn, Bacchante's head with grapes and the unknown Goddess is carrying a basket of fruit on her head. Ware in his *A Complete Body of Architecture* refers to these lively carvings as 'an acceptable rococo indulgence'. The delightful marble fireplace of Georgian proportions bears classical motifs and a

clockwise from top left:

The rococo plasterwork in the oval compartment of the staircase ceiling.

The staircase.

The ceiling in the Fisher Drawing Room.

The marble fireplace in the drawing room, now the Fisher Drawing Room.

The Victorian fireplace in the reception room of the 1853 wing, now the Symonds Music Room.

right:
Classical putti playing musical instruments. Detail from the fireplace in the Symonds Music Room.

female head adorned with wings.

The Reception Room of the 1853 wing is now known as the Symonds Music Room. The marble fireplace is Victorian save for the classical plaque of gambolling putti playing musical instruments. Both side panels have some delicate flowers, also of Victorian design. The ceiling, no longer of Palladian inspiration, has a decorative cornice with a spray of Victorian flowers in each corner of the room.

The Gothic Study, marked Study on Ware's floor plan, is a fine example of the gothic style of the 1780s. The delicate plasterwork is unlikely to be original. It strongly resembles Strawberry Hill, home of Horace Walpole, the innovator who virtually created this eighteenth-century Gothic style. Fisher used this study as his library. In his will, he left all his books to the City of Bristol Library; they included reference books on Palladian architecture.

The north-east Reception Room marked 'Dining Room' on Ware's floor plan, is in size the mirror image of the Drawing Room. However, the ceiling carvings are less exuberant; the four spandrels and the formal Palladian compartments are left empty apart from the round central panel that has an elaborate rococo design with intricate curving shapes and garlands of flowers and leaves. The fireplace has a wooden surround with a broken pediment and the classical motif of a veiled goddess.

The garden

A century after Fisher's time, John Addington Symonds recalled that June morning in 1851, when the family moved into Clifton Hill House and marvelled at the garden:

Four great tulip trees covered with golden blossoms, met our eyes… Two ponds,

far right:
The marble Georgian fireplace with wooden surround and broken pediment, in the north-east reception room.

bottom right:
The stone fireplace in the 1890 wing.

The ribbed, vaulted ceiling and finials in the Gothic Study.

The north-east reception room.

North wing reception room.

quaintly enclosed with wire railings, interrupted at proper intervals the slope of soft green turf. Each had a fountain in its midst, the one shaped like a classic urn, the other a cupid seated on a dolphin and blowing a conch.

When the gardener made the water rise for us from these fountains, it flashed in the sunlight, tinkled on the leaves and cups of floating lilies, disturbed the dragonflies and goldfish from their sleepy ways… The garden, laid out by Paul Fisher in 1747, had not been altered in any important particular, except that a large piece of it was cut away at the bottom to build a row of houses called Bellevue Terrace. [12]

The south-west gazebo.

The garden today is still the walled enclosure with a *patte d'oie* design as described on the 1746 Merchant Venturers' map of the Manor of Clifton. There are twin two-storey turrets/gazebos symmetrically positioned at the south-west and south-east corners at the bottom of the garden.

The turrets are listed in 1730 as part of the messuage of Thomas Gainer,[13] and obviously pre-date Fisher's mansion. The southeast turret is in ruins; the south-west is still used by the gardeners attached to the Hall.

They have the typical local vernacular features of oval windows on their ground floor façades and both are built of colour-contrasted Bristol Pennant stone…they are sturdily functional and there is an air of sophistication in the groin-vaulted brick roof of the lower floor of the south-west gazebo.[14]

Clifton Hill House, framed by two tulip trees.

The Palladian staircase leads onto a gravelled terrace that separates the house from the lawn. The trees and bushes are too numerous to list for the purpose of this section of the book. Of particular interest, however, are the four tulip trees (*Lirodendron tulipfera*) that John Addington Symonds mentioned and two palm trees that give a certain exotic flavour to the garden.

The only pond that survives is in great need of restoration and the valuable lead dolphin and cupid is now kept inside the House for safety.

Today, as in the eighteenth century, the commanding views over the city Bristol and beyond are breathtaking. From the perron of his Palladian staircase, Fisher could see his ships coming back laden with the imports from the West Indies on which his fortune was built. We can still see the rolling hills from Lansdown over Bath, through to Dundry, and to the east, admire the Cabot Tower and the Wills

Memorial Tower. These latter did not exist in either Fisher's or the Symonds's days.
Clifton Hill House remains a landmark in the architectural history of Bristol.

As the first truly Palladian villa conceived on Ware's scholarly designs, it remains, in Professor Mowl's words, 'a unique part of our local and national architectural heritage.'[15]

The garden after snow.

Lead dolphin and cupid from a 1920s postcard.

Notes

1 T. Mowl and B. Earnshaw, *An Insular Rococo*, p 113, Bristol, 1999.

2 *The Correspondence of Alexander Pope, 1736-1744*, Volume IV, Letter of 24 November 1739 to Martha Blount, edited by George Sherburn, Oxford, 1956.

3 H. Walpole, Letter of 22 October 1766, *Correspondence*, Volume X, p 232, edited by W.S. Lewis, Oxford, 1973.

4 Andrea Soldi, born in Florence in 1703, died in London in 1771. He began his career by painting British Turkey merchants in the Levant, and it was on their recommendation that he came to England to make his fortune in 1736. By the mid-1740s, he was so successful that it went to his head and he was 'willing to be thought a count or marquis rather than an excellent painter'. By the end of his life he was reduced to begging at the Royal Academy for charity.

5 I. Ware, *A Complete Body of Architecture*, Book III, Chapter XXII, p 405.

6 Ibid., Book III, Chapter XXII, p 406.

7 Ibid., Book III, Chapter XXIV, p 408.

8 T. Mowl, *To Build the Second City*, p 62, Redcliffe Press, 1991.

9 I. Ware, op cit., Book III, Chapter XXIV, 1756.

10 *The Letters of John Addington Symonds* edited by H.M. Schueller and R.L. Peters, Letter 1904 to Margaret Symonds, Davos, Aug 15 1891, Vol. III, p 596.

11 T. Mowl and B. Earnshaw, *An Insular Rococo*, op. cit., p 253.

12 P. Grosskurth, *The Memoirs of John Addington Symonds*, London, 1984, p 69.

13 Bristol Record Office, SMV/6/5/43.

14 T. Mowl, 'The garden at Clifton Hill House', short article, January 1992.

15 T. Mowl, 'Clifton Hill House', University *Nonesuch* magazine 2002, p 50.

Clifton Hill House: its owners and residents since 1750

Paul and Mary Fisher at Clifton Hill House: 1749/50-1762

Paul Fisher[1] was the first owner of Clifton Hill House, which was built for him between 1746 and 1750. He lived there until his death in 1762. Fisher was one of the most prominent merchants who contributed to Bristol commercial life of the eighteenth-century. Something of him is known from the factual records of his career, and from the revealing minutiae of his will. From this evidence emerges an energetic, industrious and above all conscientious man who enjoyed a reputation among his contemporaries for being extremely philanthropic and charitable. He was a great benefactor to the poor, and in 1737, he was instrumental in the foundation of the Bristol Infirmary.

Fisher was born in 1692 in the small Somerset town of Somerton, into a family of mainly apothecaries and churchwardens. His elder brother, James, was to follow in his father's footsteps as apothecary and then surgeon. Fisher probably attended the school in Somerton, which had been endowed in 1675 to teach the boys of the town and the parish. He certainly received a good education. The range of his interests, his correspondence and his library are testimony to this, quite apart from his shrewdness, which brought him fortune and respect.

Seventeenth-century Somerton had been a busy cloth-town, with many markets and fair-days, and a thriving mercers' trade. However, by the end of the century trade was beginning to decline; it was a good time to send a son to the city of Bristol. In September 1708, the young Fisher was apprenticed for seven years to Robert Smith, a prosperous Bristol mercer, and his wife Sarah. Unusually, Fisher's family agreed to provide 'his apparel of all sorts',[2] and his Master and Mistress were 'discharged there from, any custom of Bristol to the contrary thereof in any wise notwithstanding'.[3]

Nothing is known of Fisher between 1708 and the end of his apprenticeship in 1715 when he is referred to as 'Mercer and Linnen-draper'.[4] In November of that year, he was admitted to the liberties of the city with his

Indenture in Latin for Fisher's apprenticeship to Robert Smith.

friend and future nephew-in-law, Christopher Willoughby.

Willoughby was a grandson of Alderman John Willoughby of Kenn, in the Parish of Yatton; he had been apprenticed to Peter Day, a Bristol merchant of great prosperity, at the same time as Fisher was apprenticed to Robert Smith. Another descendant of John Willoughby was Mary Puxton; she and her sister Sarah had inherited a solid property from their father Thomas, a wealthy soap-boiler.

Fisher was hardworking and shrewd and his business prospered. In 1717, he married Mary Puxton. Mary's wealth was sizeable and her family was keen to protect her assets. The marriage contract stipulated that Paul was not to 'intermeddle'[5] with Mary's interests, as Paul was not himself 'possessed of any estate'.[6] Mary was worth £1,600 per annum in money and goods. The Puxtons would therefore continue to control £1,000 of this, paying the interest to Mary for her own separate use.

Fisher and his wife lived in the parish of St Nicholas where their second daughter was christened Elizabeth on 9 September 1722.[7]

Fisher's career as a merchant and linen-draper continued to flourish. His name appears in the Wharfage Books in the late 1720s when there was great expansion in Bristol, in trade, in building and in population. At first his ventures into shipping were tentative, with only a few hogsheads of goods exported each year, then increasing quantities of imports such as linens and cambrics from Dunkirk and Rotterdam, rice from Carolina, sugar and rum from the West Indies. In 1729, he was named as 'Master of the Mercers and Linnen-drapers Companie'.

By now Fisher had become part-owner of several ships: first the *Post-Boy* and then the *Scipio*, importing in greater quantities, tobacco, deer and calf skins, redwood, cotton, linen, rice, sugar, wine, rum, brandy and also trading in slaves. The early 1730s proved to be very successful and lucrative for Fisher's business. Between 1732 and 1734, together with one of his partners John King, he paid over £6,000 in duty for tobacco imports. He also became more and more involved in the thriving slave trade of the time, together with the co-owners of the *Post-Boy*, Thomas Jennys and Slade Baker, who were very active Bristol slaving agents. The *Post-Boy* entered South Carolina in August 1735 for the sale of slaves and its imports onto Bristol included 14¾ tons of redwood. Similarly, when the *Scipio* entered South Carolina in June 1736, 208 adults and 58 children were transported in and sold from the vessel. The import duties amounted to £2,333.

At the same time that he was expanding his wealth with increasing imports and the trading of slaves, Fisher was also engaged in philanthropic and charitable activities in Bristol. In 1725-26, he was Treasurer of the Bristol Incorporation of the Poor, and in 1735, he gave his full support to one new venture in the city: the creation of a much needed new hospital. Two years later, the Bristol Infirmary was founded, after 'some well-disposed persons held a meeting in which they resolved to endeavour at the establishment of a public charity'.[8] Seventy-eight persons signed, each promising to donate between two and six guineas.

This must have been exactly to Fisher's taste, son of apothecaries as he was, given to charitable work, and in company with friends and colleagues. He was involved at every stage, seventh on the list of the seventy-eight subscribers, one of the first trustees who met at Mrs Barry's Coffee-house in February 1736 to approve the new premises, and one of the committee appointed to prepare the house to receive its first patients.

The Committee agreed that the Infirmary should open on 13 December 1737. Every subscriber was summoned to meet at the Infirmary 'at 10 of the clock in the Morning, and to Dine at the Nag's Head Tavern in Wine Street'.[9] More importantly, they appointed a Committee of Nine as House Visitors. Fisher was one of the nine. He was rapidly becoming indispensable, sometimes in the chair, sometimes running the Brewing Committee, holding the keys to the Poor-box, and so on.

The Visitors took their duties very seriously, none more seriously than Fisher. A few of the nine visited the hospital nearly every day and made a report. On some days there was 'noe Complaint'[10] but the Visitors were very meticulous; on Fisher's first visit the four examined the beer 'and found it not good enough for the price'.[11]

The Visitors gave instruction for the repair of chimneys, ordered the provision of surgery boxes with panakins and a powdering tub and then instructed that £10 be given to the Matron. They recorded a 'Complaint against Robt. Clare for giving abusive language to the Nurse',[12] and sent for a kilderkin of ale to be brought in. All this in seventeen visits. Fisher was present fifteen times.

As mentioned in the previous chapter, Fisher was at the peak of his career in the 1730s; he began to look away from the 'Smoake and Stir' of Bristol to the heights of Clifton where the air was considered to be more salubrious. A few years previously in 1721, Robert Smith, the wealthy linen draper to whom Fisher was apprenticed, commissioned the architect George Tully to build Clifton Wood House. Robert

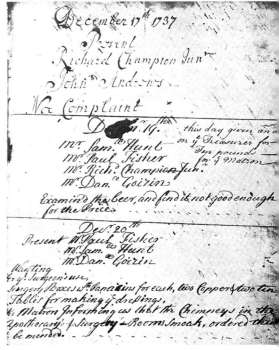

First recorded visitors' notes for the Bristol Infirmary.

Clifton Wood House.

Smith's estate of twenty acres covered the slopes below Thomas Goldney's house and included a vineyard and orchards. In 1723, George Tully also redesigned Goldney House for Thomas Goldney, the rich Quaker grocer who traded in Castle Street.

In 1735, Fisher bought the land on Clifton Hill that stretched down to Clifton Wood and the river. The same year he bought a pew in St Andrew's, the Parish Church of Clifton, paying 'the sum of five shillings a piece of lawful British money.'[13]

Before he settled in the parish, Fisher wanted to build a fine house that befitted his solid prosperity but not be pretentious. He did not choose a local builder, but turned to the London architect Isaac Ware, who designed a semi-rural house for him. Clifton was still a very undeveloped suburb in the 1750s.

At the time when this substantial piece of early Georgian architecture was erected, Clifton remained a country village. Fisher's habitation had no rivals in antiquity but the Church House and the Manor House, none in stateliness except the fine suburban villa of the Goldney family.[14]

Fisher and his wife Mary must have been able to move into their newly built house by 1750. Unfortunately, Mary was not to enjoy life at Clifton Hill House for very long. She died on 11 January 1755 as recorded in the *Bristol Weekly Intelligencer*: 'Last Tuesday died at Clifton, the Lady of Mr Fisher, an eminent Linnen Draper of this City.'

On 7 April 1743, Fisher's daughter Elizabeth married Edward Gwatkin, a wealthy soap-boiler, but she died childless before 1753.

In 1728, Fisher's brother James had died, leaving his daughter Rebecca to Fisher's care. In 1745, she married Christopher Willoughby, by then Chamberlain of the City, a widower and a colleague and friend of Fisher. A son, also called Christopher, was born in 1746, and there was a second son, Benjamin, who drowned in 1758 in one of the ponds of the garden at Clifton Hill House. *Felix Farley's Bristol Journal* of 1 April 1758 has this laconic notice:

Thursday a Son of Mr Willoughby, Chamberlain of the City, had the Misfortune to fall into the Bason in Mr Fisher's garden at Clifton, and was drown'd before he was discover'd.

During his last years Fisher continued to busy himself with the affairs of the Infirmary and the Church. He was one of the Commissioners for a new church at Kingswood and wrote to Isaac Ware to ask him to pull together Samuel Glascodine's inept plans for the tower. His own trade prospered, although in common with most Bristol merchants, he endured anxiety during the Seven Years' War.

Fisher's business was not only imperilled by war, storms, piracy, privateers, fluctuating demand and the bankruptcy of trading partners, it also posed temptations to thieves, and we find that at a Gaol Delivery held at the Bristol Newgate on 27 August 1750 one Thomas Hickes was condemned to 'be hanged by the neck until he shall be dead' for 'feloniously stealing the Goods of Messrs Fisher, Baker and Griffin to the value of 5£ in their Warehouse in this City.'

Fisher died on 4 December 1762. It was recorded in *Felix Farley's Bristol Journal* of 11 December:

St Andrew's Church, where there was a monument to Paul and Mary Fisher in the north aisle. Clifton Hill House features in the background. The church was destroyed in an air-raid on 2 December 1940.

> Saturday last died at Clifton, Paul Fisher, Esqr. He has bequeathed his House, and his Fortune which is very Considerable, to Christopher Willoughby, Esqr. Chamberlain of this City, except a few Legacies to Relations and his Servants. The Poor have lost in him a good Benefactor, as his Charity was extensive.

The bequests in the will that Fisher drew up in September 1761 were meticulously attributed and are a testimony of his concern for the poor and under-privileged as well as of his deep religious conviction. He left the organisation of his funeral to his two housekeepers:

> ...as for my body I desire it may be interred by the direction and discretion of Miss Mary Weekes and Miss Elizabeth Maunder if they or either of them shall be living with me at my death.[15]

Fisher made careful arrangements for the house itself:

> It is my Will and I do hereby direct and order my executors that good housekeeping shall be observed and kept up in my present Dwelling House at Clifton and the Garden supported and taken care of after my decease in the same manner they were kept by me while living for the Space of one whole year after my decease.[16]

There were many small bequests to friends and servants for mourning and mourning rings. Servants who did not have specific sums had a year's wages. His family in Somerton and Cork in Ireland were carefully remembered, and twenty poor families of the town of Somerton not receiving alms were to have £100 divided among them; the trustees were to be regardful of the most pious and numerous families and those who regularly attended the Church and Sacrament. He left £50 to the poor in the parish of St Nicholas under the same conditions, and the new parish of Kingswood had £300 for prayers, additional sermons, and a monthly Sacrament.

Another large bequest was of £2,000 for the Society for the Propagation of the Gospel in foreign parts. £500 of this was to establish English Protestant Schools in Ireland and £100 to be:

> Applied towards the establishment of an Episcopal see in America, according to the Principles and Usage of the present established Church in England.[17]

He left £200 to that 'Useful and necessary charity'[18] the Magdalen House in London – established for the preservation and assistance of reformed prostitutes; £300 to the Bristol Infirmary; £500 to the Mayor of Bristol in trust for a Foundling Hospital, and another £500 for a Lying-in Hospital for Poor Married Women.

As for education: £500 was set-aside for the Incorporated Society for Protestant Schools in Ireland. The new parish of Kingswood was to establish a school 'wherein poor children shall be taught to read at such hours as they could be best spared from Labour or otherwise, and instructed in the Cathechism', another £1,000 was to be:

> Applied in Marriage Portions for poor single Young Women of honest and reputable characters in the city of Bristol, in sums not exceeding £5, and was to be paid on the day

of marriage after procuring a certificate from the Minister. This would encourage marriage among the lower class of people.[19]

His library was to go to the City of Bristol. The range of subjects of his books is wide: history, theology, many collections of sermons, travel, biography and general reference. Palladio's books on architecture are there. He left his own books of devotion, his watch and personal ornaments to the younger Christopher Willoughby.

The bulk of his estate was left to his niece Rebecca and Christopher Willoughby, in trust for their son, Christopher. Fisher obviously hoped that the then 16-year-old boy would marry and settle down at Clifton Hill House.

In a codicil of November 1762, Fisher wrote:

> I desire the said Christopher Willoughby the Elder and his Wife to dwell until my said Heir shall attain to the age of twenty four years and in such House I order the like Number of Servants to be employed and kept both for the Garden and otherwise as I myself used to do and I desire that my said House shall be kept together with the Garden in neatness and Decency by them as hitherto hath been.[20]

In spite of this, neither the elder nor the younger Christopher ever moved to Clifton Hill House. The association of Clifton Hill House with the tragedy of the drowning of their son, Benjamin, must have been too painful for Christopher Willoughby and his wife Rebecca. The family stayed in their house at 43 Prince Street where Christopher the elder died in 1773.

Christopher Willoughby the younger first moved to Berwick Lodge in Hallen, and then bought the estate of Marsh Baldon, near Abingdon in Oxfordshire, where he could continue more expansively the farming life he enjoyed. His daughter Juliana was christened at Marsh Baldon in 1777. Rebecca, his widowed mother, moved in with him and is recorded in Marsh Baldon church as having died in 1799.

Christopher became a famous agriculturalist, forward-looking and enthusiastic. For his work he was granted not only a baronetcy in 1794, but also a D.C.L. from Oxford. Arthur Young has much to say in his praise in his *General View of the Agriculture of Oxfordshire* of 1813 for his innovative and successful practices in farming.

The Eltons, the Crosses and the Bushes: 1776-1832

Advertisement for the auction sale of Clifton Hill House and cellars in May and June 1830.

Christopher Willoughby the younger disposed of his interest in Clifton Hill House and its estate shortly after his father's death in 1773. It is probable that by 1776 Clifton Hill House was the home of Edward Elton (1746-1811). His house in Clifton was described as a 'messuage together with fixed grates, venetian blinds', three coach houses, three stables and a garden.[21] Edward's wife died in 1780 leaving him with six children under the age of eight and this may have induced him to move to a more manageable house in Clifton, particularly as he neglected his own business interests, which included shipping, coal, sugar, olive oil, copper, banking, the Bristol Crown Fire Office, and his office in George Street to attend to his wife's extensive business interests, which frequently took him away from Bristol. By 1786 Clifton Hill House was the residence of James Cross, a wealthy distiller, formerly of 7, Temple Cross,[22] who served as church warden of the parish church in 1790-91, and the *Bristol Directories* show a Mrs Sarah Cross resident there from 1793 to 1822 when Robert Bush, merchant, moved to Clifton Hill House from 30 College Green where he is listed as pewterer.[23]

Bush came from a family of staunch Tory merchants. In 1785, he traded from 20 High Street and was a 'member of the firm of coppersmiths trading in the city at the end of the eighteenth century as Robert Bush and Co. He was elected Mayor in 1795 and declined to serve and again in 1810 with the like result.'[24] Bush was President of the Gloucestershire Society in 1809. He was Master of the Merchant Venturers Society in 1823-1824, and President of the Dolphin Society in 1825.

Bush died on 4 March 1829, aged sixty-seven. His son George is listed as resident at Clifton Hill House in 1830 in *Matthews's Annual Bristol Directory*. On 3 June of the same year, according to the *Bristol Gazette*, Clifton Hill House was to be sold by auction. The auctioneer, Mr Fargus, also mentioned Bush's well-stocked cellars for an earlier auction at the end of May 1830. Judging by Mr Fargus's description of the excellent wines, 'Old Port, Sherry, Rum and Cider' and others, Bush must have been a real 'bon viveur'.

Clifton Hill House was still the most important mansion on Clifton Hill. The house, garden and stables, were rated at over £160 in the property assessment of the Clifton Lighting and Watching Rate of 1829. This was the highest rating on Clifton Hill, higher even than that of Goldney House at £140.

George Eddie and Mary Sanders: 1832-1851

George Eddie Sanders[25] was born on 1 August 1778, the third son of Thomas Sanders the Elder of Bristol and Sarah. George was born in St Thomas Street, Bristol and christened in the parish church of St Thomas the Martyr on 31 December 1779.[26] Together with his two elder brothers, Thomas Sanders and John Naish Sanders, he was educated at a school run by Mr John Exley, a well-known local mathematician and author of *Principles of Natural Philosophy, or a New Theory of Physics*, published in 1829.[27]

Thomas Sanders the Elder died in 1801 and in his will he left the family business to his eldest son Thomas, and expressed the particular wish that he would bring his two brothers into the partnership.[28] This he did and soon John Naish Sanders and George Eddie Sanders were active members of Thomas Sanders & Co, of 2 Bridge Parade, Bristol. As soon as he attained his majority George became a Freeman of the City of Bristol, a role he appears to have taken very seriously as local politics would soon play a major role in his life.

Thomas Sanders & Co were seedsmen, corn and hop merchants. They were wholesalers of corn and hops for the millers and brewers of Bristol but also traded in seeds of all types, including exotic plants from far-flung countries that they then supplied to the local nobility.[29]

Along with his brothers, George had many interests outside of the family business. His brother Thomas Sanders, together with Richard Reynolds and Susannah Morgan (a close friend of Josiah Wedgwood) founded the Prudent Man's Friendly Society in 1812.[30] This organisation was to be the first attempt at creating a savings bank in Bristol and had three objectives: the suppression of mendacity, the creation of a 'loan fund' for the industrious poor and the creation of a 'fund for savings' to encourage the labouring classes to lay up in store whatever they could manage to meet future adversity and old age. The first two of these objectives were purely eleemosynary in character and maintained by donations from benevolent inhabitants of Bristol and Clifton, whilst the third was totally distinct and self-sustaining from its commencement.

George Eddie Sanders was a generous contributor to the fund but also joined with his brothers in a further, more intellectual activity when they joined together to promote a Philosophical and Literary Society for Bristol.[31]

Portrait of John Naish Sanders, brother of George Eddie Sanders.

The Bristol Library Society (established 1772) found itself to be lacking space in 1808 and entered into an agreement with the Philosophical and Literary Society to erect a new building for their joint use. A committee was to be formed and members of both societies would buy shares in the new building. However, before the new building could be completed the Library Society, feeling its existence threatened, decided to withdraw from the project.

The success of the building project was assured only by the generosity of shareholders like John Naish Sanders and George Eddie Sanders. To assure the long-term survival of the project it was thought necessary to establish in 1823 an institution for the advancement of science, literature and the arts, which would have its own museum and library. The Philosophical and Literary Society continued as a separate body, but associated to the Institution.

After the death of George Eddie Sanders in 1851, it was again proposed that the Library Society and the Institution should merge, and in 1871 the two organisations amalgamated to become the Bristol Museum and Library. The original building at the bottom of Park Street was sold to the Freemasons and remains today the Hall of the Provincial Grand Lodge of Bristol.

In the summer of 1807, George Eddie Sanders married Maria Hannah Bishop, daughter of Samuel Wilson Bishop a London merchant who had retired to Oxford. The wedding took place in Oxford where the bride was still residing with her parents at No.1 Holywell Street. Maria Hannah was sister to the Reverend Henry Bishop of Oriel College. Henry Bishop sat on the Parliamentary Commission at the time of the 1832 Reform Act. In the 1851 census the Reverend Henry Bishop is recorded as living with George Eddie Sanders, only three days before Sanders died.[32]

We do not know exactly when George and Maria married but it would seem from his will and those of their relatives that they did not have any children.

In 1810, we know from surviving deeds that he was owner and lord of the manor of Kingston Seymour in north Somerset, about fifteen miles from Bristol.[33] From the local census records it appears George sold his interest in the manor some time before 1841. As he first appears at Clifton Hill House in 1832 it is possible he disposed of his interests in his Park Street and Kingston Seymour properties in order to finance the acquisition of his new home.

From contemporary writings we know that George began his political life as a Tory but converted relatively early to the Liberal cause. He was then active as a

Liberal councillor for many years in central Bristol and member of the Bristol Liberal Executive Committee. George Eddie Sanders was a Liberal councillor for the Redcliffe Ward in 1835, 1836, 1839 and 1840 and for the Bristol Ward in 1846, 1849 and 1851 (when he died in office). In 1818 he was elected, but declined to serve, as President of the Colston Society. He sat on the Finance Committee and the Dock Committee of the Corporation of Bristol. In 1826 he was also a Magistrate for the City of Bristol and for the County of Gloucestershire.[34]

In his role as Justice of the Peace he was a visiting magistrate for the Bristol Pauper and Lunatic Asylum. Contemporary magistrates included his friends and family, notably: Nicholas Roch, Abraham Hilhouse, John Scandrett Harford, William Fripp and John Naish Sanders.

The Bristol Charity Trustees were formed as a result of the 1835 Municipal Corporations Act and George Eddie Sanders served from 1836-1851 as one of the first of twenty-two trustees alongside Samuel Brown (1836-1850), Charles Bowles Fripp (1836-1849) and Thomas Powell (1836-1872).

George was also a member of the provisional committee of the proposed Bristol, Northern and Western Railway Company in 1824.

After many years campaigning with his colleagues for a better water supply in Bristol he was appointed chairman of the Bristol Water Works in 1840.

George Eddie Sanders died on 2 April 1851 at Clifton Hill House.[35] Maria had died ten years earlier; her will was witnessed by Dr Symonds.

The Symondses: 1851-1880

This represents the longest period of occupation of Clifton Hill House as a private residence. It stretches over the two generations of Dr John Addington Symonds and his son, also named John Addington Symonds. They were both Victorian figures of great stature and their lives are well documented.

Dr Symonds lived at Clifton Hill House from 1851 until his death in 1871. Born in Oxford in 1807, he came from a Puritan Nonconformist background and an unbroken line of many generations of doctors and surgeons. As a boy he attended Magdalen College School in Oxford. In 1825, he went to Edinburgh to study medicine and took his M.D. in 1828. Back in Oxford he helped in his father's practice until 1831, when he moved to Bristol at the instance of his uncle John Addington

Dr Symonds at Clifton Hill House.

right:
Dr Symonds as a young lecturer at the Bristol Medical School in 1840, by Joseph Swayne, the then 15-year-old medical student.

Mary Ann Sykes, 'Auntie'.

Mlle Girard; Charlotte and John Addington Symonds's Swiss governess.

Symonds of Ashley Court. Dr Symonds was the first physician to be appointed at the Bristol General Hospital and became the first Lecturer in Forensic Medicine at the Bristol Medical School. In 1836, he was appointed Lecturer in the Practice of Medicine, a post he was to hold for the next seventeen years.

Dr Symonds was also a poet of some standing, writing poetry in the early hours of the morning before he dealt with his medical affairs, hiding his poetical talents from his patients for fear of being regarded as frivolous.

In 1834, Dr Symonds married Harriet Sykes, a beautiful but delicate Bristol girl. The couple had seven children, of whom only four survived to adulthood. They lived first at 15 Park Street, then 7 Berkeley Square, where Dr Symonds also had his medical practice, until the family moved to Clifton Hill House in June 1851. By that time Dr Symonds was a prominent, influential and fashionable doctor. He was elected to the Royal College in 1853. Harriet died of scarlet fever in 1844, whereupon her sister, Mary Ann Sykes, moved into Clifton Hill House to help her widowed brother-in-law rear his four young children and to receive guests at the house. Though she was somewhat puritanical, Mary Ann Sykes was described by the Symonds children as having a great sense of humour. However, she never quite replaced the mother that the young John had lost when he was just four, and as he later noted in his memoirs:

> She was essentially kind, but neither just nor tender – variable in temper, nervous and timid in her dealings with my father… Her position as head of our family without being either mother or wife was a very difficult one.[36]

Dr Symonds was also helped in bringing up his children by Mademoiselle Girard, the Swiss governess, to whom John Addington Symonds felt very close. Mademoiselle Girard brought some light relief to the household and enjoyed playing games with her charges. Symonds said she was a natural teacher, and taught him the little German he knew. She joined the Symonds family in 1853 and probably stayed at Clifton Hill House until the early 1860s.

Soon after he moved to Clifton Hill House, Dr Symonds added a wing to the southern side of Fisher's Palladian villa. The date 1853 is inscribed on the stonework. The room, now known as the Symonds Music Room, provided another grand reception area where Dr Symonds liked to entertain the literary and artistic élite of his time. On these occasions the house was filled with distinguished and talented people like Lord Lansdowne, Lord Macaulay, Dr Jowett, Henry Hallam, John Percival (first Headmaster of Clifton College), John Sterling, Thomas Woolner and Jenny Lind, the celebrated 'Swedish Nightingale'. She sang several times at the Victoria Rooms[37] in Clifton. In 1862 she stayed at Clifton Hill House and sang in Dr Symonds's drawing room.

Margaret Vaughan, Symonds's third daughter, wrote in *Out of the Past*: 'This may seem almost inconceivable, but I have constantly heard it repeated as a fact in my Father's family. Jenny Lind sang on so high a note that one of the fine Venetian glasses on my grandfather's mantel-piece fell shattered to small atoms!'[38] Margaret Vaughan also wrote:

Jenny Lind.

> In this new home [Dr Symonds] began to place his ever-increasing possessions – the collection of prints and pictures in the fine portfolios, the glasses and books and carpets such as persons of his tastes loved to surround themselves with in the Victorian era. Did the Nonconformist ancestors come and 'walk' in that splendid drawing-room so richly caparisoned with all the things they had themselves adjured?[39]

A watercolour by Catherine Symonds shows the main reception rooms as they were around 1867. It is a family scene showing the old Dr Symonds together with Janet, John Addington Symonds's eldest daughter born in 1865, for whom Edward Lear wrote 'The Owl and the Pussy Cat' and 'The Duck and the Kangaroo' among other 'nonsense poems'. It also shows Dr Symonds's important collection of paintings by Renaissance masters, and classical objects.

At the time of his death in 1871, Dr Symonds was 'not only perhaps the greatest and best-beloved physician in the West of England, but one of European reputation.'[40] He was hailed as the doctor of the Poor and of the Rich known by the name of 'Good Physician', not only amongst the fashionable crowds of Clifton, but also in the farms and lanes and country houses within a radius of many miles around.[41]

Dr Symonds was omnipresent in and around Clifton. His obituary in 1871 reads:

Reception Rooms at Clifton Hill House circa 1867: watercolour by Catherine Symonds.

> He seemed to be the daily companion of each of us, so certain were we when we stepped out of our house or even looked out of our windows, to see Dr Symonds and his carriage…His well-horsed Brougham always proceeding at a tearing pace, was a well

The reception rooms after 1871 with the William Morris wallpaper.

Portrait of John Addington Symonds around the time he moved to Clifton Hill House, by the local artist Vigor, whose studio was situated at Royal York Crescent.

known object in Clifton.[42]

Symonds's son-in-law, Sir Edward Strachey, wrote after his death about his medical proficiency as well as the breadth of his interests:

He had reached the highest knowledge and skill as a physician; …none had attained to more of the science and the art of medicine; and if he had not preferred Clifton to London, no name would have been more eminent than his in the profession…But while the practice of medicine was the real work of his life, there was no subject of human interest, of which his active mind did not take thoughtful notice. Art, poetry, history, science, philosophy, and politics in their oldest and newest form…[43]

Soon after his father's death, John Addington Symonds, true to his promise, moved into the family house where his wife Catherine swiftly tried to remove some of her father-in-law's oppressive Victorian clutter, and introduced a fashionable William Morris wallpaper in the main reception rooms.

Symonds was born at 7 Berkeley Square on 5 October 1840. He grew up in his father's highly cultured and intellectually stimulating household. He recalled in his memoirs:

The ease in which we lived, the number of servants who waited on us, the carriages and horses, the large house and its profuse objects of interest and beauty, the dinner parties we gave and the crowds of distinguished people who visited our home.[44]

He met many of the famous Victorians with whom his father was acquainted.

Symonds's early childhood was probably not a very happy one. His mother died when he was four. His memories of that time are dominated by the figure of his formidable maternal grandmother. She was the leader of the Plymouth Brethren in Bristol. The group met in her house in Cornwallis Crescent. Symonds recalled:

It was a motley crew of preachers and missionaries, trades-people and cripples…all gifted with a sanctimonious snuffle, all blessed by nature with shiny foreheads and clammy hands, all avid for buttered toast and muffins… She [Symonds's grandmother] held the most innocent amenities of life for sinful…She delighted in the Lamentations of Jeremiah...she used to chant those lugubrious verses, which began or ended with Thus saith the Lord: woe, woe to the ungodly.[45]

Symonds was a sickly and hypersensitive child, given to alarming night terrors and suffering from many physical ailments. 'I fancied there was a corpse in a coffin under my bed, and I used to wake up thinking it had risen and was going to throw a sheet over me.'[46] However, in spite of his fragile constitution, he seems to have been an eager pupil. He was taught Latin by his puritanical paternal grandfather before the age of five, then attended a small private school in Buckingham Vale, Clifton until he was sent to Harrow to be, according to his father, 'made a man'.

The ethos of the school did not suit his temperament nor did it stretch him spiritually or intellectually. He was deeply homesick and kept referring to Clifton Hill House and its garden, asking his beloved sister and faithful correspondent, Charlotte, to send him leaves from the copper-beech tree at the bottom of the garden.

Symonds treasured some very fond memories of the time in June 1851 when the family moved from Berkeley Square to Clifton Hill House:

John Symonds at Harrow.

On that eventful morning, I entered the solemn front door, traversed the echoing hall, vaulted and floored with solid stone, and emerged upon the garden at the further end. An Italian double flight of balustraded steps, largely designed, gives access to the gravelled terrace which separates the house from the lawn. For us it was like passing from the prose of fact into the poetry of fairyland…This transition from Berkeley Square contributed greatly, I am sure, to make me what I am…I am certain that the new [home] formed my character and taste at a period when youth is more susceptible. My latent aesthetic sensibilities were immediately and powerfully stimulated.[47]

From Harrow, Symonds went to Balliol College, Oxford: 'My first feeling upon coming up to Balliol in the autumn of 1858 was one of relief.'[48] Symonds was in his element at Oxford. His intellectual powers were stretched to the full in the company of such academics as Dr Jowett, the Master of Balliol College, Professor John Conington, Matthew Arnold, and Professor T.H. Green, the philosopher.

Mental growth was rapid…I devoured literature of all sorts with avidity; and when I was tired of history, philosophy, and the classics, I composed in verse and prose for my

Charlotte Symonds, beloved sister and faithful correspondent.

John Symonds at Oxford. Years marred by ill-health and mental exhaustion.

Symonds's letter about 'The Owl and the Pussy Cat'.

own amusement, or else read poetry and studied pictures.[49]

He proved to be a brilliant student at Oxford. In 1860, he was awarded the Newdigate Prize for an English poem on 'The Escorial' as well as the Chancellor's Prize for an essay on 'The Renaissance'. He also became Fellow of Magdalen College. However, in spite of his academic achievements, Symonds's years at Oxford were marred by ill-health and mental exhaustion, often exacerbated by the increasing awareness of his homosexuality and the difficulty of coming to terms with what was unlawful in Victorian society. He left Oxford in 1863, soon to settle in London and enter the legal profession.

All his life Symonds would be prey to a succession of bouts of depression, mental torment and exhaustion alternating with periods of intense literary production. After a few years in London training as a lawyer, Symonds and his wife Catherine settled back in Bristol at 7 Victoria Square to be near Symonds's father. Ill-health compelled him to give up the legal profession and he devoted himself entirely to literature and scholarly pursuits. The winter months he would spend in Europe, often for health reasons or simply for pleasure. The Symondses had always been great travellers, spending nights in trains and days visiting churches and art galleries or climbing the glaciers of Mont Blanc. In 1867, Dr Symonds diagnosed his son as having a serious lung disease, and on his advice, Symonds and his wife wintered at Cannes. There they often met Edward Lear, whom Catherine knew from her childhood as a close friend of her father's, Frederick North, the MP for Hastings. Symonds wrote:

Mr Lear comes here nearly every day and it was with him that I sprained my ankle. And nearly every day he brings Janet[50] a fresh picture or poem – a portrait of The Blue Bird or The Red Bird – illustrations of Sing a song of Sixpence …One original song about The Owl and the Pussy Cat who went to sea & travelled & got married she is very fond of & has by heart.[51]

Cannes represented a turning point in Symonds's emotional development. He suffered the throes of a physical and mental breakdown and even contemplated suicide but 'emerged at last into Stoical acceptance of [his] place in the world, combined with Epicurean indulgence of [his] ruling passion for the male.'[52] It was the first step towards Symonds's self-acceptance and sexual liberation. He bravely disclosed to his young wife his irrepressible attraction to the male sex. The couple were then able to find a sort of modus vivendi, Catherine showing a dignified resignation and an affectionate understanding towards Symonds's proclivities.

> The anomaly of my position is that I admire the physical beauty of men more than women, derive more pleasure from their contact and society, and am stirred to sexual sensations exclusively by persons of the male sex.[53]

The Clifton years, from 1870 to 1877, saw a remarkable literary output. *An Introduction to the Study of Dante, Studies of the Greek Poets,* and the first three volumes of *Renaissance in Italy* were published in spite of many journeys abroad and more bouts of ill-health. Symonds also continued to give sixth-form lectures on Greek literature at Clifton College. It was here that he met the fifteen-year-old Horatio Brown and struck up a lifelong close friendship with him.

While at Clifton Hill House, Symonds was very active on the local scene and fulfilled many civic duties: 'I was elected to my father's place upon the Council of Clifton College…. I helped to found the Bristol University…. I acted as secretary to an Invalid Ladies' Home at Clifton and sat on the Committee for promoting the Higher Education of Women.'[54] Thus, Symonds was pleased to report a preponderance of young ladies when University College opened in October 1876:

> Bristol University College opened yesterday with a lecture on History from Mr Rowley. There were perhaps three young men & about fifty female students…This shows that the work of our Association for the Higher Education of Women has really done something for the place.[55]

In June 1877, after months of ill-health and mental overwork, Symonds suffered a dramatic lung haemorrhage. His friend, the Clifton doctor John Beddoe, persuaded him to seek out more clement climes, and the Symonds family decided to winter in Egypt. However, they broke their journey at Davos in Switzerland, where instead of Egypt, Symonds chose to settle more permanently as the quality of the air and the climate proved remarkably beneficial to his health. He joined a community of a thousand or so invalids plagued with tuberculosis and other debilitating lung

Portrait of Janet, the Symondses' eldest daughter for whom Edward Lear wrote 'The Owl and the Pussy Cat'.

Horatio Brown.

Am Hof in Davos, by Catherine Symonds.

ailments. This was the time when Dr Ruedi, the world authority on consumption, and a small group of German doctors were experimenting with the simplest of treatments: mainly rest in the open air during the hours of sunshine together with a healthy diet chiefly of milk, cod liver oil and a small quantity of alcohol. 'The only thing relied upon is air....the worst symptoms of pulmonary sickness – fever, restless nights, cough, blood-spitting, and expectoration – gradually subside by merely living and breathing'. Peregrinations abroad in search of health were not new for Symonds, but at no time hitherto had he thought of a permanent exile. However, the Alpine climate proved so beneficial to his health that it was soon decided to leave England for good. Thus, in August 1880, the family travelled back to Bristol to break up and empty the old family home, Clifton Hill House. Ruthlessly and stoically they burnt the family papers, the letters, the diaries of seven generations.

In *Out of the Past* Margaret Symonds wrote:

The old house was fearfully full of possessions in my Father's time, for his family were distinctly hoarders. Amongst other things they hoarded letters. That strange, unobtrusive race of Nonconformist doctors….rarely destroyed a letter…We children helped in the general devastation; and to us it was also a form of orgy. Every morning we all assembled in the study and sat ourselves down in a circle. My Father opened the boxes and the drawers and threw on the floor the letters, the cash-books and the diaries. There were hundreds and thousands of them, and we tore them across with childish delight…
As we went on tearing, tearing, huge piles of paper, high as an Alpine avalanche, rose up around us. The gardener and the groom came backwards and forwards with big clothes-baskets which they stuffed with torn paper, and carried… down the garden paths to a place where the weeds were always burned on Saturday afternoon beneath a clump of elms. Here the baskets disgorged their contents on a smoking bonfire, and when we grew tired of our tearing in the study, we joined the gardener and the groom and danced round the burning heap, poking at it with long sticks. The letters curled and quivered, the damp and ancient desks unclosed, showing old pictures of people long

since dead, old pieces of tape and green labels – old trophies of a smouldering long-forgotten, never to be resurrected past….When the papers were done with, my Mother had her way with the busts of all those unlovely emperors and philosophers such as our grandfathers duly bought on their 'grand tours' and stuck up in their halls or book-shelves to depress both themselves and their children with for ever after. My Mother had a large trench dug in the garden, and the busts were all wheeled down in wheelbarrows and put in the trench, and then the earth was shovelled in, and then my Mother got in herself and danced upon the earth. She was indeed an heroic young lady, for all that happened fifty years ago; and people didn't destroy their family trophies at that period, and certainly they did not dance on them.[56]

Davos became the family's new home, and Symonds spent the rest of his life between Davos and Italy, coming to England only at very infrequent intervals. After some years spent at the Davos Hotel Pension Buol, the family finally moved in September 1882 to Am Hof, the new house that Symonds had built:

in a big meadow of that name. It was the first house in that broad hayfield – a pleasant sunny place, full of field flowers….Am Hof was designed to combine a certain amount of English comforts with all the wise appliances acquired by centuries of good Italian and Swiss architects… The planning and the building of our future home was a great joy to us as children, and we were all running across to see how it progressed… All our masons were Italian – but the inside fittings of the house, the panelled walls, the parquet floors, the simple but hand-made furniture, were all fashioned by two good local carpenters.[57]

The west and south fronts of the house had long wooden balconies, so that Symonds could benefit from most of the hours of sunshine, breathing the pure Alpine air.

It seems that in Davos the Symondses were able to enjoy the comfortable life style to which they were accustomed at Clifton Hill House, in England. The household at Am Hof ran smoothly with the help of two parlour maids who remained in Catherine's service for twenty years, a governess and nurses for the Symonds daughters, and M. Bérard, the very skilled and highly paid French chef. There were also kitchen maids and ordinary housemaids, soon to be joined by Angelo Fusato,[58]

Symonds reading on the balcony in Davos.

Handsome gondolier Angelo Fusato, Symonds's devoted companion and servant.

Symonds with the Swiss peasants.

Symonds's gondolier-cum-valet, footman and companion, whom he met in Venice in 1881.

The family would usually spend several of the spring months in Venice, and would travel with most of their servants. Margaret Symonds recalled in *Out of the Past:*

That wonderful spring when we made our first journey to Venice we took him [M. Bérard] with us. We had taken the piano nobile of the Palazzo Gritti on the Grand Canal,..we had our own beautiful gondola; we had all the pictures, all the lagunes and all the churches, and we had Mons. Bérard to cook for us. But M. Bérard, too, had the pictures and the churches. One afternoon he arrived in our great Salone with a look of tragedy on his melancholy features: 'I leave you,' he cried, 'it is impossible for me any longer to spend hours with Titian, Bellini and Veronese, and then return to my casseroles. If I stay another hour I shall throw myself down from the summit of the Campanile!' M. Bérard packed his bags and departed. We found him, however, awaiting our return at Am Hof.[59]

Palazzo Gritti today.

In Davos, J.A. Symonds enjoyed consorting with the lower classes, the Swiss peasants, the local artisans; he felt he could achieve that universal male comradeship cutting through social and cultural strata of the kind that Walt Whitman was advocating. In fraternising with his fellow human beings Symonds was following Walt Whitman's teachings that convinced him of the 'absolute equality of men.'

He was mentally and physically revived not only by the quality of the High Alps air, but also by the overwhelming beauty of the scenery. He felt at one with nature. At times, though, like R.L. Stevenson, who was his neighbour for over two years, Symonds could feel a prisoner of his surroundings and experience boredom and melancholy in an ocean of snow: '…life at Davos has become for me a permanent sort of tunnel…which is a gallery in the middle of a marble-hard avalanche, fifty feet beneath the frozen air of Alpine winter in a stony ravine.'[60] However, unlike R.L. Stevenson who left Davos for warmer climes, Symonds never, for the sake of his health, contemplated moving out of Davos.

He integrated himself wholeheartedly in the local community and he came to be regarded as an unprecedented asset to the town's development. He financed the building of the Davos Gymnasium and founded the Davos Gymnastic Club. He delighted in the spectacle of the young athletes' brawny and healthy bodies as well as the harmonious mixing on an equal footing of the sons of bankers and landowners with clerks and artisans. Symonds also helped local businesses and hotels thrive and pioneered today's Winter Sports at Klosters. He presided over the Davos Winter Sports Club and Toboggan Club. In 1889, he initiated the first Davos International Toboggan Race. He believed that sport was one way to bond nations and that this race 'down the post road to Klosters'[61] would allow 'people of all tongues to compete once a year'.[62]

Symonds giving the 'Symonds Cup' in Davos, 27 January 1885.

Davos still remembers Symonds and has a street named after him near Am Hof which is now divided into flats.

Symonds's literary output in Davos was also remarkable: the last four volumes of *Renaissance in Italy, The Life of Michelangelo*, an essay on Shelley, and another on Elizabethan Drama, several volumes of verse and lengthy works of translation including the Italian: T*he Sonnets of Michelangelo Buonarroti*, and *The Life of Benvenuto Cellini.*

In Davos, Symonds kept abreast with what was happening in England through his prolific correspondence and regular visits from his many friends. He particularly enjoyed the company of Robert Louis Stevenson and the intellectual and stimulating conversations they had during the two winters in the early 1880s that Robert Louis Stevenson spent in Davos with Fanny and Lloyd Osbourne. Though Symonds was at first rather condescending towards Stevenson, he soon realised that this younger writer was something of a genius. 'So gracious and pure a light has never fallen across my path as fell from this fantastic and yet intensely human genius – the beautiful comradeship of the Shelley-like man, the eager and gifted wife – the boy to whom the world owes *Treasure Island*.'[63]

Symonds occasionally travelled back to England to see his publishers, and frequently went to Rome and to Venice, where he had a pied-à-terre. He loved meeting people from all walks of life from gondoliers to aristocrats, and he enjoyed many casual sexual encounters. Symonds was particularly attracted to young handsome working-class males like Christian Buol, the bi-sexual Swiss sledge-driver, with

Symonds sledging at Klosters. A photograph now displayed in the Symonds' Library.

Robert Louis
Stevenson.

Symonds in
Davos.

Symonds in
Venice.

whom he had a lasting relationship.

Symonds was determined to bring about pressure to change the law against homosexuality and more particularly to have the Labouchère[64] Amendment repealed. He felt that homosexuality should be studied scientifically, and in *Sexual Inversion* which he wrote with Havelock Ellis, he presented many case histories, including his own. In this respect, Symonds was ahead of his time in campaigning for more liberal attitudes towards homosexuality. He is regarded as a pioneer of the twentieth-century gay movement.

The impact of Symonds's writings on homosexuality would have been much greater if they could have been published in their entirety, but the climate of the age and his family's sensitivities unfortunately played a negative part in the years following his death.

In his will, Symonds entrusted Horatio Brown with all his literary papers, autobiography, manuscripts, diaries and letters. Symonds's papers were to be published at Brown's discretion but nothing would be published without Catherine's permission. This was a promise that Symonds made to Catherine, undoubtedly to spare her feelings, in the last and barely legible letter that he wrote to her on his deathbed. It is a poignant reminder of the deep affection that bonded them. Catherine was herself ill with typhoid fever in Venice:

> There is something I ought to tell you, and being ill at Rome I take this occasion. If I do not see you again in this life you remember that I made H. F. Brown depositary of my printed books…I do this because I have written things you could not like to read, but which I have always felt justified and useful to society. Brown will consult and publish nothing without your consent.[65]

This amounted to a 'mission impossible' for Brown who was forced to omit much of Symonds's writings about the 'Problem', as well as about homosexuality in general. Brown published a sanitised biography of Symonds in two volumes in 1895. The pressure to discard potentially embarrassing writings also came from Symonds's sons-in-law. They feared the scandal that would follow the revelation of Symonds's homosexuality, knowing this would greatly jeopardize their position in society. On their insistence, the second edition of Havelock Ellis's *Sexual Inversion* did not mention Symonds as the co-author.

There was a further incident in the late 1920s, a few years after Brown's death, when more of Symonds's papers were burnt out of the same fear of outrage and scandal. In his book *Venice Rediscovered*, Dr John Pemble gives a remarkable analysis of the tragic loss of Symonds's papers: 'With the destruction of Brown's archive were lost not only many details of Symonds's life but a unique record of that network of homosexual relationships and sympathies whose existence, while so difficult to prove, is yet crucially significant in the history of Britain from the mid-Victorian age until the 1930s.'[66]

Symonds died in Rome on 19 April 1893. The world of literature was in mourning; he was, said the *Saturday Review*, 'a high priest in the temple of Literature...' The French critic Paul Desjardins devoted a whole page in *Le Journal des Débats* of April 1893 to Symonds's life and works. He hailed him as a major figure in the world of literature and art history.

Symonds was more than a man of letters; his complex personality, his life and work were re-assessed one hundred and five years to the very day after his death, at a Symposium held at Clifton Hill House in April 1998. This international symposium brought together leading authorities in the field of nineteenth-century art and literature. A compilation of the papers given at the Symposium was edited by Dr John Pemble under the title *John Addington Symonds, Culture and the Demon Desire,* published by Macmillan in 2000. Phyllis Grosskurth, Symonds's twentieth-century biographer, was the guest of honour at the symposium. She unveiled a plaque in memory of Symonds at 7 Victoria Square, where he lived from 1868 to 1871.

Catherine Symonds, John Addington Symonds's life-long companion deserves a special mention. She was born in 1838, the younger daughter of Frederick North, MP for Hastings.

Symonds and Catherine met at Mürren in Switzerland in 1863. In his diary Symonds described her as 'dark and thin and slight, nervous and full of fun and intellectual acumen,' and her sister, Marianne North as 'blonde, tall, stout, good-humoured, and a little satirical...Both the young ladies were devoted to sketching.'[67] Symonds fell in love with Catherine's 'earnest vivacity',[68] and they were married a year later at Hastings in November 1864:

It was a brilliant wedding; for Mr North, as Member, was much beloved; and irrespec-

Phyllis Grosskurth unveiling the Symonds' memorial plaque at 7 Victoria Square, Clifton.

Catherine Symonds in Rome 1882.

John Addington Symonds and Catherine North's wedding, Hastings, November 1864.

tive of the town, the whole countryside including the Duke of Cleveland, came to do us honour.[69]

The marriage was a mixed blessing; sexually it seems to have been a total failure in the absence of 'a strong sexual attraction on either side'.[70] However, four daughters were born of this union. Catherine suffered greatly from serious bouts of depression during and after her pregnancies. She would sink into sombre moods, unable to lead a normal life, obviously suffering from what is now defined as post-natal depression. The couple decided to abandon all sexual intimacy soon after the birth of their fourth daughter, Katharine, in 1875. This arrangement suited both parties:

…I separated from my wife with her approval. She gave it readily; for the sexual side of marriage had never been for her more than a trouble… I do not repent the line we took. It placed me upon a sound and true relation with my wife – that of pure and faithful friendship, which from the commencement had been the real basis of our union.[71]

Catherine Symonds's sketch of the garden at Am Hof, 1897.

They remained devoted to each other as they also were to their children. 'The children are the nicest things belonging to us now',[72] Catherine wrote in 1871 to her friend Mrs Clough. From descriptions by her daughters Madge and Katharine emerges the portrait of an attentive, tender mother whose 'vast common sense'[73] always helped solve their problems. 'She fulfilled her woman's life as a wife and mother to the uttermost.'[74]

As head of two households, Clifton Hill House and Am Hof, Catherine always treated her servants in a kind and efficient manner. She was the ideal mistress. 'Regularity of meals, light and sunshine in the whole house. Smiling faces amongst the maids. Kindness and mutual respect between master and maid and guests.'[75]

Like her elder sister, Marianne North, Catherine was a very talented artist whose passionate love of nature in general, and flowers in particular, is evident in the many watercolours she painted. Like Edward Lear, William Holman Hunt was a friend of Catherine's father and a frequent visitor at Hastings Lodge, the North family home. He had a great influence on both girls in the art of drawing and painting.

Catherine outlived Symonds by twenty years; after his death in 1893, she spent a few more years in Davos before selling Am Hof and returning to England. Switzerland soon faded into the realm of memories. Back in England she first moved to

Lyme Regis before settling at Camberley with her recently-widowed daughter, Katharine Furse. She delighted in her grandchildren and the growing of flowers in her garden. She died in Oxford in 1913 aged seventy-five.

The Symondses's daughters

Catherine and John Addington Symonds's four daughters all lived at Clifton Hill House for at least part of their early childhood.

Janet (1865-1887) sadly died of tuberculosis in Davos aged only 22. She seemed to have been blessed with a gentle personality.

> She was the saint in our family and from the date of her birth she appears as such in all the records…during the years of her illness we all looked to her for spiritual leadership.[76]

Charlotte (1867-1934), or Lotta as she was known to her family, married Walter Leaf the distinguished Greek scholar, Chairman of the Westminster Bank and a governor of Marlborough College. She had a highly sensitive nature coupled with a great sense of responsibility.

> She was the socially-minded member of our family, enjoying dancing and skating, and had a beautiful voice and in many ways excelled her noisier and rougher sisters.[77]

Dame Katharine Furse, G.B.E., Director of the W.R.N.S., in her uniform.

below left:
The three surviving sisters in London, 1898.

Diana of the Uplands, Charles Furse.

Distant view of Kangchenjunga from Darjeeling, India. Marianne North completed over 200 paintings during her visit to India in 1877-79.

Margaret (1869-1925), known as Madge, was born in Clifton. She was the closest to her father; she shared his passion for art and literature, and was a gifted writer in her own right. She was with her father when he died in Rome. She married William Wyamar Vaughan, Headmaster of Wellington and Rugby Schools who was cousin to Virginia Woolf. She became a close friend of the Stephens girls, later on known as Vanessa Bell and Virginia Woolf, and was the inspiration for the character of Sally Seton in *Mrs Dalloway*. Madge could have played an important part in the 'Bloomsbury circle', had it not been for her egotistic, jealous and intolerant husband who deemed the group immoral and strongly disapproved of them. Madge published several books including *Out of the Past* but her husband thwarted what could have been a successful literary career.

Katharine (1875-1952) was the youngest and the most remarkable of Symonds's daughters. She was born at Clifton Hill House but spent the majority of her formative years in Davos and in Italy. She was a kind of free spirit, a sheer individualist with a tomboy disposition and an irrepressible need for independence. Her education in the schoolroom at Am Hof was left to governesses or to her parents, and was unusual and often unorthodox. In her autobiography and collection of family memories, *Hearts and Pomegranates*, published in 1940, she recalled that when she was seventeen she felt the need for a more formal education. Accordingly, she was sent for a very short time to the Mont Fleuri boarding school in Lausanne. The only subjects that she enjoyed were practical ones such as Home Nursing, Anatomy and First Aid; these were to stand her in good stead later, in her V.A.D. days.[78] In 1917, Katharine with her indomitable energy was instrumental in the creation of the Women's Royal Naval Service. She was appointed Director and received the honour of Dame Grand Cross of the British Empire in the same year. In 1928, she became Director of the World Bureau of Girl Guides and Girl Scouts.

In 1900, Katharine married a friend of John Singer Sargent, the painter Charles Wellington Furse. Furse, like Sargent, excelled in society portraits as is illustrated by the painting of his wife as 'Diana of the Uplands'.[79] They had two sons, Peter and Paul who both went into the Navy. Charles died in 1904, thus ending a marriage that:

had proved to be satisfying in every way, and we hoped for a future full of creative work which would established Charles more firmly as one of England's leading artists.[80]

Katharine was keener than her sister Madge to investigate their father's sexuality and tried to shed more light on 'the problem'. In 1939, Virginia Woolf urged her to 'let the cat out of the bag'.[81] Unfortunately 'she [Katharine] died in 1952, without having published any study of her father...None of the evidence she had collected survives in her papers, and the truth is now beyond recovery.'[82]

Marianne North, known as Aunt Pop by the Symonds family, was a regular visitor at Clifton Hill House, and is also worth a special mention. She made her name as the highly-regarded Victorian botanist who left to the nation her remarkable collection of oil paintings of the flora and fauna she studied all over the world. Nature was her 'vision of Eden'.[83] Her beautiful paintings are imbued with poetry and scientific precision. Queen Victoria and Charles Darwin were among her admirers and supporters.

Distraught after the death of her beloved father in 1869, she began, at the age of almost forty, exploring faraway lands. She was intrepid and unusually adventurous for a woman of her age and social class, travelling often on her own to Japan, Indonesia, Sri Lanka, Brazil, the United States, India, New Zealand, Australia, the Seychelles, Jamaica and Chile. There is a parallel with the art of Edward Lear who painted exotic birds and foreign landscapes with the same attention to detail.

Marianne North left her botanical paintings to the Royal Botanic Gardens at Kew. The Gallery there was designed under her personal supervision to display 832 of her botanical paintings, and was opened to the public in 1882. It is a unique pictorial record of tropical and exotic plants of every continent she visited over almost twenty years. The panelling is fashioned from the 246 different types of wood she collected on her travels. She also wrote some fascinating accounts of her travels and the people she met.

In 1877, in Ceylon, Marianne North met another remarkable Victorian woman, the photographer Julia Margaret Cameron.

After her peregrinations across five continents, Marianne North settled down in 1885 to live in the village of Alderley in Gloucestershire, in an old house surrounded by a large garden. She devoted herself to radically transforming her garden, introducing some of the rare species of flowers and plants that she had encountered in her journeys across the world. Sadly, she was by that time weakened by years of gruelling travels, having suffered exposure to harsh and unhealthy climates, as well as poor diets. Her severe deafness and the disturbing 'voices' that were haunting her,

Marianne North at her easel in an exotic setting.

Marianne North as a gypsy by the photographer Julia Margaret Cameron.

Mr. W. J. Rogers.

William John Rogers.

PERCY ROGERS

President of the Dolphin Society. Chairman of W. J. Rogers, Ltd. Captain of West Gloucestershire Polo Club, and hunts with the Berkeley Hounds. Served in R.N.V.R. during war. Educated Harrow and Oxford; captained Balliol Rowing Club and helped twice to win Ladies' Challenge Plate at Henley, '90 and '91. Rowed 2 in Trial Eights in '91.

He'd play upon the harp a solo;
Than play upon the harp a solo;
He'd rather go to Failand golfin'
Than wear a "topper" for the Dolphin.
But still with smile and jocund jest
We know he'll do his level best
To beat, I know the nut's a hard 'un,
The record made by Captain Mardon.

Caricature of Percy Rogers.

plagued the last years of her life. She died on 30 August 1890. Symonds wrote her epitaph which can still be read on the sun-dial in her garden at Alderley. Her sister Catherine Symonds edited her *Recollections of a happy life: Being the autobiography of Marianne North* in 1892.

The Rogers: 1882-1909

In the summer of 1880, following the burning of the family papers and the disposal of the contents of the old home, Clifton Hill House was to be let or sold. In *Out of the Past*, Margaret Vaughan recalled first seeing the eventual tenant, William John Rogers and his wife:

> People came to look over the house. We eyed them with great distaste… After the raising of a good many objections by the smiling lady and her husband, who objected to the carpet beating on Brandon Hill, the old house was eventually taken by them, and a few weeks later we left our first home, never again to return to it.[84]

As Symonds himself wrote: 'I feel confident that Rogers means to take my house, unless negotiation spoils his temper.'[85]

William John Rogers must have moved into Clifton Hill House with his family from Heathside in College Road, around 1882. He lived at Clifton Hill House until his death in December 1908. Undoubtedly, like the Symonds, the Rogers would have entertained friends and clients in the house. As already noted in a previous chapter, Rogers built the northern wing which added a large reception area to the house.

By the 1880s, Rogers was a very wealthy maltster and brewer.[86] In 1852, already trading in Old Market Street as a maltster and rum merchant, he acquired the nearby Jacob Street Brewery. Within twenty years he rebuilt the brewery and turned it into one of the most successful in the south west.

Rogers was one of the first to see the potential of the Great Western Railway for a trading 'corridor' and soon exploited it by having a tied estate of public houses in South Wales and a distribution depot in London. The Rogers had three sons: Arthur Stanley, Tracy Percival and Herbert. Coincidentally the second son, Percy, like John Addington Symonds, was educated at Harrow and then at Balliol College,

Oxford. Later on, the sons acted under their father as co-directors of the Brewery.

> Mr Rogers is most particular as to the quality of the raw materials used, and is careful to select only those that possess particular qualifications for special brewings.[87]

Rogers had his own maltings, he built a 300-feet-deep well that was reputed to be the deepest in Bristol, and had a filtration tower and massive cellarage.

> Mr Rogers…brews large quantities of special ales for London and country bottlers, who are supplied from the brewery with labels bearing Mr Rogers' specially registered 'Monarch Brand'.[88]

The Rogers Brewery on Jacob Street.

Rogers registered the business on the Stock Exchange in 1894, and expanded his chain of public houses, engaging architects to design them. Two notable ones are the Garrick's Head in the centre of Bristol (since demolished), and the Cambridge Arms in Coldharbour Road, Westbury Park, Bristol.

Rogers's Brewery was massive, and half had to be demolished to make way for the Temple Way underpass in the early1960s. Luckily a listed portion still survives as Company House, it is next to the Pip 'n Jay Church opposite the Bristol Evening Post building. A contemporary noted of Rogers that '[he] took no active part in public life, although he has been invited to accept the highest municipal honors.'[89]

According to a short obituary notice in the *Bristol Times and Mirror* of 23 December 1908, William John Rogers died on 22 December at Clifton Hill House. Rogers's brewery continued to thrive under the direction of W.J. Rogers' sons until the 1930s when it was bought by Simonds of Reading.

The Rogers name has long been associated with Bristol with some really notable persons amongst them; one Rogers was a fabulously wealthy soap-maker and Lord Mayor, and another was Woodes Rogers, the famous privateer and Colonial Governor, the man who rescued Alexander Selkirk.

Rogers' Monarch Ale.

Notes:

1 In writing this part of the chapter the author has drawn on the research carried out by Miss Sheila Brennan, formerly Warden of Clifton Hill House, and is indebted to her.

2 Bristol Record Office, 'Paul Fisher, Apprenticeship to Robert Smith, 23.9.1708', Reference 09467 (i).

3 Ibid.

4 Bristol Record Office, 'Burgess Books'.

5 Bristol Record Office, 'Bond of Marriage of Paul Fisher and Mary Puxton, 18 January 1717', Reference 09471/14/c.

6 Ibid.

7 St Nicholas Parish Registers, P/St./R/1(j).

8 G. Munro Smith, *A History of the Bristol Royal Infirmary*, p 6, Bristol, 1917.

9 Ibid., p 24.

10 Ibid., p 27.

11 Ibid., p 27.

12 Ibid., p 27.

13 Bristol Record Office, 'Indenture of 25 May 1735', Reference 09467 (6b).

14 P. Grosskurth, *The Memoirs of John Addington Symonds*, London, 1984, pp 67-68.

15 Bristol Record Office, 'Paul Fisher's Will, Sept. 16 1761', 39304/4, PROB 11/884.

16 Ibid.

17 Ibid.

18 Ibid.

19 Ibid.

20 Ibid.

21 The sale particulars of the house in the *Bristol Gazette*, announcing the auction on 3 June 1830 mention 'a double coach house, six-stall stable, gig house, and harness room' which approximates to the three coach houses mentioned by Edward Elton half a century before.

22 *Sketchley's Bristol Directory* 1775 (Kingsmead Reprints, Bath, 1971), p.22; Merchants' Hall, Bristol, Box 8/a, Bundle No. 5, lease from the S.M.V. of Dean's Close and Honey Penn Hill Field to James Cross, dated 25 May 1786. Cross was President of the Grateful Society in 1776 and died 27 June 1791, The Revd A. B. Bevan, op. cit., p. 337.

23 *Matthews's Bristol Directories* for 1825 and 1829 and the Clifton Lighting and Water Rate Books show that Robert Bush the Elder was resident there from 1822, until his death on 4 March 1829, aged 67.

24 *Bristol Times and Mirror*, April 29 1907.

25 Richard Sanders, descendant of the Sanders family, kindly wrote this article on the G.E. and M. Sanders at Clifton Hill House.

26 Bristol Diocese Baptismal Registers – Vols. 11 to 14: Index and Transcripts 1754 to 1812.

The Marianne North Gallery at the Royal Botanic Gardens, Kew.

27 Published by Longman, Rees, Orme, Brown and Green, 1829.

28 Will of Thomas Sanders, proved at London in 16 December 1801 – PROB 11/1367.

29 Letter from Thomas Sanders to the Marquis of Lansdowne dated Bristol 2 February 1801.

30 *The Rules, with a Short Explanation of the Views of the Prudent Man's Friend: A Society Established in Bristol at a Public Meeting Held in the Guildhall, on 22 of December, 1812,* printed by M. Bryan and sold by Barry.

31 Bristol Institution for The Advancement of Science, Literature and the Arts, c 1808-1871 – Ref: 32079.

32 1851 Census of Clifton.

33 Somerset Archive and Record Service – Kingston Seymour DD\SOG/693 1810.

34 National Archives – C 202/225B/9.

35 *The Gentleman's Magazine* – May 1851.

36 P. Grosskurth, *The Memoirs of John Addington Symonds,* p 67, London, 1984.

37 The Victoria Rooms, a grand neo-classical building designed by Charles Dyer in 1832, is now used suitably as the Music Department of the University of Bristol.

38 M. Symonds (Mrs Vaughan), *Out of the Past,* p 18, London, 1925.

39 Ibid., p 14.

40 Ibid., p 7.

41 Ibid., p 9.

42 H. Reid, *A Chronicle of Clifton and Hotwells,* Redcliffe Press, p 80, 1992.

43 *Miscellanies by John Addington Symonds, M.D., Selected and edited, with an Introductory Memoir, by his son,* pxxviii, London, 1871.

44 M. Symonds (Mrs Vaughan), op. cit., p 80.

45 Ibid., p 17, 19.

46 H. F. Brown, *John Addington Symonds, A Biography,* Vol. I, p 10, London, 1895.

47 Ibid. pp 40, 41, 45.

48 Ibid. p 101.

49 P. Grosskurth, *The Memoirs of John Addington Symonds,* op. cit., p 122.

50 Janet was Symonds's eldest daughter, born in 1865.

51 *The Letters of John Addington Symonds* edited by Herbert M. Schueller and Robert L. Peters. Letter to Mrs Clough of 22 January 1868, Vol. I, pp 791-792.

52 P. Grosskurth, *The Memoirs of John Addington Symonds,* op. cit., p 173.

53 Ibid., p 65.

54 H. F. Brown, *John Addington Symonds, A Biography,* op. cit., p 72.

55 The Clifton Association for the Higher Education of Women was started in February 1868 on the initiative of John Percival, the first Headmaster of Clifton College and a close friend of Dr Symonds. Young lady students could follow courses of lectures on a great variety of subjects. Symonds was a regular lecturer for the Association and described as 'a brilliant and inspiring personality'.

56 M. Symonds (Mrs Vaughan), *Out of the Past,* op. cit., pp 186-7.

57 Ibid., pp 189, 190.

58 Angelo Fusato, though a married man (his wife became one of the Symonds's servants in Am Hof), was a devoted companion to Symonds. In recognition of his services, when Symonds died, he was left an annuity by the family until his own death.

59 Ibid., pp 191-192.

60 *The Letters of John Addington Symonds,* Letter of 11 May 1888, from Venice to Henry Sidgwick, op. cit., Vol. III, p 305.

61 M. Symonds (Mrs Vaughan), *Out of the Past,* op. cit., p 201.

62 Ibid.

63 Quoted in a 1926 review in the *Daily Mail* of Margaret Vaughan's recently published book *Out of the Past.*

64 Labouchère (1831-1912) was a journalist and Liberal politician. In 1885, the 'Labouchère Amendment' criminalized all sexual contact between men in Great Britain and remained on the books until 1967. Oscar Wilde and Alfred Taylor were sentenced under this amendment.

65 *The Letters of John Addington Symonds*, Letter to Mrs Catherine Symonds, op. cit., Vol. III, p 839.

66 J. Pemble, *Venice Rediscovered*, p 68, Bristol, 1995.

67 M. Symonds (Mrs Vaughan), *Out of the Past*, op. cit., pp 137-138.

68 Ibid., p 137.

69 Ibid., p 156.

70 Ibid., p156.

71 P. Grosskurth, *The Memoirs of John Addington Symonds*, op. cit., pp 260, 261.

72 M. Symonds (Mrs Vaughan), *Out of the Past*, op. cit., p 157.

73 Ibid., p 304.

74 Ibid., p 163.

75 Ibid., p 306.

76 K. Furse, *Hearts and Pomegranates, The story of Forty-five Years, 1875 to 1920*, op. cit., p 21, London, 1940.

77 Ibid., p 81.

78 V.A.D.: Voluntary Aid Detachments that Katharine was instrumental in setting up during the First World War. She had previously joined the Red Cross and worked with the British Expeditionary Forces as a volunteer nurse. She became Commandant-in-Chief of the British Red Cross.

79 *Diana of the Uplands* by C.W. Furse, A.R.A. is at Tate Britain, London.

80 K. Furse, *Hearts and Pomegranates*, op., cit., p 218.

81 J. Pemble, *Venice Rediscovered*, op., cit., p 69.

82 Ibid., p 70.

83 *A Vision of Eden, The Life and Work of Marianne North* is the title of the book published in collaboration with the Royal Botanic Gardens, Kew. HMSO., 1980.

84 M. Symonds (Mrs Vaughan), *Out of the Past*, op. cit., p 188.

85 *The Letters of John Addington Symonds* Letter of 23 August 1880 to Henry Dakyns, op. cit., Vol. II, p 647.

86 In the writing of these pages the author is indebted to Mark Steeds of the Bristol Long John Silver Trust and owner of the Beaufort Arms at Hawkesbury Upton, for his professional knowledge of the Rogers Brewery and for his ready willingness to share it. His help has been invaluable.

87 A. Barnard, *Noted breweries of Great Britain and Ireland*, p 330, 1891.

88 Ibid.

89 W.T. Pike, *Bristol in 1898-1899: Contemporary Biographies* Vol.1, p 162.

A University Hall of Residence: 1909 to the present time

In 1909, Clifton Hill House was bought by the University of Bristol to become its very first Hall of Residence. University College, Bristol had opened in October 1876 with two professors, five lecturers and ninety-nine students. It was the first institution of its kind to admit men and women on an equal footing: this was at the insistence of Dr Jowett (Symonds's Master at Balliol and a frequent visitor at Clifton Hill House) who, with John Percival and John Addington Symonds, was instrumental in the establishment of the University College.

In 1907, Miss May Christophera Staveley was appointed to lecture in history and be tutor to the women students of University College, Bristol. Miss Staveley:

> ...believed that the fullness of a University life can be best realised in residence, and she soon kindled to action others who saw the need for a Hall for women students living outside Bristol.[1]

The House and Gardens in the 1910s.

In November 1908, thanks to Miss Staveley's persistence, a committee was formed that included influential members of the Fry and Wills families. When Clifton Hill House came on the market in 1909, Miss Staveley, almost recklessly, used all her powers of persuasion to induce the Committee to buy it. As Margaret Vaughan recalled in her memoirs:

> In 1909 my mother sold Clifton Hill House and also the house adjoining it – Callander House[2] – to Bristol University to be used as a hostel for the women students of the new University. Both my mother and father were eager pioneers in the Women's Higher Education Scheme, and I can imagine no better destiny for that old house of many memories.[3]

Dr Jowett (*left*) and Dr Percival.

A generous and anonymous donation from two ladies, who had no connections with Bristol, enabled the House to be bought for £5,500. These two ladies were friends of Miss Staveley's. They were very keen supporters of women's education

The academic staff of University College, Bristol in 1909. Miss Staveley, lecturer in History and Women's Tutor, is seated second from left.

Four of the first fifteen students in 1911 in the common room.

as well as being eager to save old beautiful houses and their gardens from greedy developers. Thus, in September 1909, after somewhat hasty preparations, the first fifteen women students took up residence. As E. Butcher put it:

> True, there were not enough wardrobes or mirrors to go round, but these were mere trivia: the Hall of Residence was a living fact.[4]

In March 1911, Catherine Symonds came back to visit Clifton Hill House with her daughter, Margaret Vaughan, who later wrote in her memoir *Out of the Past*:

> The young lady students of Bristol University live in that great drawing-room today. They pin the lists of their common-room on the white partition walls. Some of my Mother's beautiful sketches are hanging where once the Guido Reni and Caracci copies hung...[5]

Catherine herself wrote to Katharine, her youngest daughter, that her return to Bristol seemed like a dream when she visited their old home:

> I saw and admired the stately old rooms, turned into cubicles for students (one of them black!). Then, last night I went to a real 'gemüthlich' small dinner at the kind Abbots where my dear old friend Lewis Fry, had come back all the way from his sister's funeral at Saltburn in Yorkshire to meet us. The talk was of Bristol University and the wheedling manoeuvres by which Major Abbot had got £100,000 to start it, out of Sir W. Wills, the only really rich man in Bristol. How well I remember, 20 years ago, when your father and Doctor Percival went forth on the same quest, and were treated with contumely and scorn everywhere by the half rich citizens who did not believe in education!.. Now Bristol is beginning to be proud of its university, and it is its great topic of conversation everywhere.[6]

In July 1911, Callander House and also an adjoining nursery garden were sold by Catherine Symonds, for the sum of £4,000. The purchase by the University was again made possible by the help of the same friends, who once more, insisted on complete anonymity. Callander House was still tenanted at that time,[7] but Miss Staveley had plans for extending the building, as the demand for residence by women students was growing significantly every year. She contacted the firm Oatley and Lawrence as early as 1913. 'Miss Staveley was always the inspiring spirit, and never ceased planning for the improvement and usefulness of the Hall and its surroundings.'[8] However, the plan was put in abeyance by the outbreak of the First World War. Work force and building materials were in short supply and the Ministry of Munitions refused permission for any extension to Callander House until 1918 when eight new bedrooms were built above the 'Gym'. The Gymnasium created on the site of the stable, and the addition of a veranda from the garden to the Hall, were the gifts of Dame Mary Monica Wills in 1913 and 1914.

The Clifton Hill House students in summer 1911.

In 1919-20 another generous gift from the Wills family enabled the stable-yard to be transformed into a dining room that could accommodate the now 40 residents. (See 'Restoring the House: 1988 to 2009') In the space of ten years the Hall had grown from fifteen women students to forty, and numbers were constantly on the increase. G. A. Wills, Treasurer of the Hall Committee for 17 years, also financed the creation of the new wing in Callander House and its complete redecoration, again in 1919-1920.

During Miss Staveley's wardenship some famous visitors stayed at Clifton Hill House, as is recorded in an early visitors' book: Dame Clara Butt, Charlotte Green (Symonds's sister), the Poet Laureate, John Masefield who stayed at Clifton Hill House in October 1914 and again in 1922. Dame Clara Butt's flamboyant autograph dwarfs those of John Masefield, and Charlotte Green who visited in May 1923.

Visitors' Book with the autographs of Clara Butt, John Masefield and Charlotte Green.

The First World War brought great changes to the University itself, as well as to the Hall:

In the almost complete absence of men students, the women had to keep the student societies and sports going as far as possible, and those in Hall plunged into this energetically, as well as into such wartime tasks as keeping the garden, the grass tennis court and nets in some sort of order when no gardener was available.[9]

The Gymnasium.

Two students dressed for tennis, 1918.

Students and staff in 1918-1919.

A student bedroom around 1920.

Acting was also a favoured activity at the time. Miss Barry joined the Hall as early as 1910 as Secretary to Miss Staveley. She took an energetic part in the budding amateur dramatics with performances of *Comus* in the summer of 1914, and *Twelfth Night* in 1917 performed in the garden with an all-female cast. Miss Barry became Sub-Warden in 1918. In 1938 she encouraged the foundation of the Clifton Hill House Dramatic Society.

By the 1930s, the Hall had again grown in size and could welcome some forty-five students. During the Second World War, under Miss Macleod's wardenship the Hall also accommodated twenty-four students evacuated from King's College, London. By the time France was defeated, Bristol was beginning to experience night-time raids. Clifton Parish Church, opposite Clifton Hill House, went up in flames on 2 December 1940.

> A few nights later, the Warden [Miss Macleod] had to use several Minimaxes on the rafters of Callander House to save it from a like disaster.[10]

To deal with the increasing night air raids, the University introduced fire-guard duties to be carried out by young men students. This was a very popular innovation at Clifton Hill House:

> When the war was over, the Senior Student recorded the Hall's regret for the loss of the lively and entertaining company of the permanent fire watchers who had become so much a part of the Hall.[11]

During Miss Macleod's wardenship the Hall expanded greatly, as did the University at large: in 1956, Goldney House was acquired and its first students became part of Clifton Hill House. Clifton Wood House was similarly added in 1957 and ran as part of Clifton Hill House until 1999 when, after an inspection from the fire authorities, it was deemed unsuitable for multi-occupancy. Sadly the University sold Clifton Wood House – a delightful eighteenth-century building – instead of funding the work to comply with the necessary fire regulations.

In 1960, Miss Macleod presided over the construction of Fry Wing; the *Evening Post* devoted a special report to the ambitious building programme of the University of Bristol.

The new wing was named after the Fry family who have been connected with the University since the nineteenth-century. The family crest of three horses can be seen below the pediment of the main front door. The pediment and the hewn stone work somewhat echo the nineteenth-century Gibbs surround of the entrance of Clifton Hill House.

Fry Wing was regarded at the time as a 'state-of-the-art' building with solid wood built-in furniture in study bedrooms, a large common-room with a student bar named the Three Horses, and improved catering facilities in a large and airy new dining hall. Some 120 rooms and tutors' flats were created. Fifty years on, the Fry Wing has been renovated as well as budgetary constraints permitted; the Symonds Library was created out of a large ladies' cloakroom, some larger kitchen areas where students can socialise replaced the antiquated laundry rooms. However the study bedrooms and the bathrooms do not meet the expectations of twenty-first century students and conference delegates.

In 1972, a very unimaginative new building, South Wing, was erected and provided an extra 72 study rooms with the luxury of a wash basin in each room. Since 1972 there have been no other building works but a major renovation and restoration programme was started in 1988 and continues to this day.

Miss Macleod and the Clifton Hill House Committee 1945-46.

A photograph of the students taken on D-Day. The four young men at the back were the Clifton Hill House firewatchers.

The main entrance of Clifton Hill House with the Fry family crest.

The 1972 South Wing.

Clifton Hill House today

As present Warden of Clifton Hill House I would like to give an insight into what life is like at Clifton Hill House nowadays for residents and the staff who work there. When I reflect on my wardenship, now spanning twenty-one years, I think it has been a truly unique experience. Like Miss Staveley I feel I have put my heart and soul in the role. The post of warden, for which there is no training course or diploma, is a job with no defined hours of work. Apart from fire alarms being set off accidentally or intentionally by students at night, crises often happen outside 'normal' working hours. With 230 students in residence, it is likely that accidents will occur, psychological traumas will have to be dealt with immediately – all this in addition to the inevitable anxieties from which students can suffer in striving to cope with the demands of their chosen course of study.

The role of Warden requires flexibility, tolerance, common sense, understanding, patience and humour. Only a matter of weeks after I took over in 1988, a kitchen trolley was 'kidnapped' and held in a secret location. The kidnappers removed a wheel from the trolley and threatened continuing mutilation of this hapless 'victim' unless the quality of the food in Hall was improved. Clearly their demands were met as, in 1994, the student newspaper *Epigram* declared Clifton Hill House the best catering hall in town!

Obtaining a place at university is a great achievement and opens the way to self-discovery as well as discovery of others. However, it is not unusual for students to be apprehensive, stressed and even depressed, especially at the beginning of their university career. Freshers' Week is the first hurdle to conquer. Students have to adjust to an unfamiliar environment without the comforts of home, trying to make friends, striving to fit in. This can create tensions as not all are inclined to fall in with the 'binge drinking' culture which prevails in society at large and in some student circles.

Acclimatising to university life is not infrequently complicated by home events. Parents often wait for their child to go to University before separating, or moving house, or both, and these events can cause immense traumas to their offspring. On such occasions wardens and their team are called upon to give support, comfort and encouragement. The pastoral care we give our students is equal to none and I am confident that many students owe their degrees partly to the help they receive from their wardens when they are struggling with personal or academic problems. Our pastoral care is even more important for students with special needs, physical and/or mental, who would find it practically impossible to cope at University were it not for the very safe environment provided by the Hall community. Special attention is also given to overseas students who stay in Hall during the Christmas and Easter vacations. They are often invited to share our family Christmas meal.

It is always gratifying to see how much students change in their first year in hall. They become more confident; some will have acquired skills by having responsibilities in the running of the Junior Common Room; others will have learnt independence and the ability to coexist with their peers to everybody's advantage. It is unlikely that a year spent in a 'bed-sit' would have achieved as much!

Clifton Hill House has a balanced mix of home and foreign students representative of the University community as a whole. The Hall reflects in number and gender the different academic departments; it provides a variety of social, cultural backgrounds, religious beliefs, and gives all students a unique, enriching and worthwhile experience that facilitates scholarship and offers a full civilised and civilising life. Most Bristol students have outstanding potential that is encouraged to flourish not only in their chosen disciplines, but also through the many activities and social events that take place within the Hall calendar. Clifton Hill House has always had a lively community of musically talented students who organize concerts and 'playathons' (24 hours non-stop piano playing in the JCR) several times a term, for various local, national and even international charities as diverse as the Meningitis Trust, the Teenagers' Cancer Trust, Saint Peter's Hospice, the Pachod and Puna Health Centre in India, to name but a few.

From the time of its becoming a Hall of Residence under Miss Staveley's leadership, Clifton Hill House succeeded in developing a strong sense of community and loyalty to the Hall that students often call their second home. Much of this ethos has remained to this day. The sense of belonging through Hall activities and personal relationships is developed within a smaller unit than the University at large, especially at a time when 'contact teaching hours' in departments are shrinking significantly.

Friendships that are formed often last a lifetime. Many students come back and visit, invite us to their weddings and give us family news when children are born. Some met their future partners in Hall and subsequently married and are always

The twenties' garden party.

top:
The 2008 Halloween Formal Dinner.

above:
An invitation to the 1991 Christmas Ball.

proud to come back to Hall to show off their offspring.

The Hall is a community, much like a very large family, and domestic animals can be prominent members just as in any household. A cat called Charlie lived in Hall for almost 20 years, feared by some and loved by others. Because of his unpredictable temperament he was always treated with caution and respect. He was even given a mention in the 2002 Year Book: 'Charlie rules the corridors with an iron paw, slashing and biting through anyone or anything that gets in his way!' Pablo, the Sub-Warden's cat, and 'adorable Dora', the receptionist's white poodle, remain as the Hall pets and are the object of much affection with our students.

Hall life would not be possible without the hard work of our wonderful Supporting Staff (previously known as domestic staff). They are very tolerant, caring and understanding of the young students they look after.

Members of the Junior Common Room and Senior Common Room also play a major role in the successful running of the Hall. The Junior Common Room members represent the student body. They are a useful link with the Hall staff and Senior Common Room. They also run the Bar where students socialise in the evenings and during Hall events.

The team of Tutors greatly help students with pastoral and academic issues. They keep a watchful eye on the students of their respective corridors, helping and guiding students with all events and making sure that health and safety requirements are adhered to and budgets are not overspent.

The first big event of the academic year is the 'Halloween Formal' on 31 October. It is followed in December by the memorable Christmas Ball which, in the last few years, has been known as 'The Snow Ball' with the 'Survivors' photograph taken after the walk back from the Suspension Bridge and the Champagne breakfast in the Hall dining room.

The Valentine Formal Dinner is always very popular and well attended. It is usually followed by the Clement Wheeler-Bennett Convivium. In 1986, Clement Wheeler-Bennett, a Clifton Hill House student reading Economics and Politics, tragically died of cancer. In his memory, his parents set up a 'Convivium' that takes the form of an evening when current students at Clifton Hill House, the Chancellor, Vice-Chancellor, academics from different departments, the Lord Mayor and various Bristol dignitaries, are invited to attend a talk by a distinguished speaker who has excelled in life, and afterwards enjoy a wine tasting together. The very first Convivium was organised by Clement's friends and contemporaries in 1987. From a very modest gathering in the first few years following Clement's death, the Convivium has grown in size and stature. It is now one of the most important events in the Hall Calendar. Speakers have included Lord Armstrong of Ilminster, Professor Sir Joseph Rotblat, Kate Adie, Lord King, Alastair Fothergill, Ann Widdecombe, Peter Lord, Dr Adam Hart-Davis and Professor Angellini. The Nobel Peace Laureate, Professor Sir Joseph Rotblat, deserves a special mention: in 1999, aged over 90, he delivered a 45-minute talk without notes, about his role in the development of the atomic bomb and his subsequent conversion to the cause of abolishing nuclear weapons. On the night, Professor Rotblat was given a standing ovation by a spellbound audience.

The Hall Garden Party, organised in June by the newly elected JCR, is the highlight of the Summer Term. It is usually based on a theme, and students have to come up accordingly with imaginative ideas for the appropriate costume to wear, dressing up as Romans, or gangsters or in the fashion of the twenties.

The Hall also maintains a well-established tradition of amateur dramatic productions, pantomimes and musicals being performed every term.

In the early nineties *Romeo and Juliet*, *A Midsummer Night's Dream* and *The Taming of the Shrew* were produced in the main garden and attracted many local residents who enjoyed alfresco suppers before the performances. The Clifton Hill House Music Group of the nineties became the Clifton Hill House Performing Arts Society in 2006, and produced the musical, *Copacabana*, in November that year.

In 1999, a memorable performance of *The Boyfriend* received a standing ovation in the Junior Common Room, and again in 2006 when all the guests were invited to wear 1920s clothes. *Fame*, *Joseph and the Amazing Technicolor Dream Coat*, *My Fair Lady*, *Guys and Dolls*, *Anything Goes* and *Grease* have been among the most popular performances of recent years.

The ninetieth anniversary of Clifton Hill House as a hall of residence was celebrated with a carol concert followed by a very successful formal dinner attended by former students, including Mrs Phyllis Mattock, Mrs Mary Williams, both residents in the mid-1920s, Mrs Joan Hughes, resident in the 1930s, Miss Evelyn Libra,

Professor Sir Joseph Rotblat and Annie Burnside, Warden, 1999.

The Boyfriend, 2006.

My Fair Lady.

resident in the 1940s and Mrs Ann Stark, resident in the 1960s. A well-attended reunion was organised in 1996 to celebrate the creation of the association SCHH (Students of Clifton Hill House) by Ellie Stark and Howard Dellar. SCHH was a continuation of the CHHOSA that had stopped recruiting new members.

In the early nineties I made the Hall study bedrooms strictly non-smoking long before it became a legal requirement; and in 1998 I also enforced the non-smoking rule in the JCR and bar. This was not welcomed by everybody but had been the wish of many students working in the Bar and suffering from passive smoking.

Clifton Hill House will soon be celebrating its centenary as a Hall of Residence; it has changed over the years but has retained a sense of continuity in the way it has been run. It has always been more than a mere institution; it has nurtured and helped generations of students at the start of their university careers. It is today a lively community of some 230 students whose lives, like John Addington Symonds's, are in some ways shaped and influenced by their time in this historical house.

Paul Fisher's lasting legacy was the erection of Clifton Hill House, one of the most important Palladian villas in the south west of England. By the stipulations in the last part of his will, Fisher was expressing the hope that his house and gardens would be lived in and well looked after following his death. In many ways, his wishes have been met. Clifton Hill House and its gardens have been lived in and well looked after almost continuously since his death in 1762.

Biographical notes on the Clifton Hill House Wardens

May Christophera Staveley 1909-1934

Miss Staveley, whose drive and determination led to the acquisition of Clifton Hill House by the University of Bristol, was born in 1863 into a Quaker family in Wisbech, Cambridgeshire. She was the fourth daughter of Eastland Staveley, a schoolmaster, and his wife Ann, and was educated mainly at home. In 1895, she went up to Somerville College, Oxford to read Modern History. Hilda Oakeley, one of her contemporaries at Somerville wrote:

> She brought a spirit of nature with her as she came towards us, tall and swift and radiant, with a halo of golden hair, her sea-blue eyes which deepened in the earnest defence of good causes, her face expressing strength and sweetness and utter sincerity.[12]

After graduation, she went to Birmingham to become the first warden of its Women's University Settlement. In 1905, she became head of the Women's Hall of Residence at Liverpool University, and lecturer in History. She became known for her work for women's causes. As already noted, in 1907, she took up a similar appointment at University College, Bristol. Later on, as a member of Somerset Education Committee she became a governor of the Sidcot Quaker School and was also president of the Bristol Branch of the Federation of University Women.

Miss Staveley was well-known for her strong dislike of smoking, especially smoking in women, and her love of animals. She was hardly ever seen without her King Edward spaniel and Pekingese dogs, and Bobby, her long-lived parrot.

She was remarkably caring for and supportive of the girls under

Miss Staveley, in 1917, with four students and Bobby the parrot on the terrace.

her charge; she also liked to keep in touch with past students, often working into the night answering their letters.

When Lewis Fry of Goldney House died in 1921, legend has it that she vetoed the plan to make Goldney the first hall of residence for men because of its proximity to Clifton Hill House. In fact it would appear that the opposition instead came from G.A. Wills and Professor Lloyd Morgan, the first chairman of the Hall Committee.

Mr Wills was so 'strongly of opinion that Goldney House should not be used for men students, owing to its proximity to existing Halls of Residence for women students' that he promptly gave £30,000 to establish the men's Hall (Wills) at Downside.[13]

Miss Staveley's wardenship spanned a long period of time and profound social changes, from the Edwardian era through the First World War to the Depression of the 1930s. She devoted most of her life to the running of Clifton Hill House. She gave the Hall its foundations and her belief that halls of residence should be 'an academic community of people that should value and facilitate scholarship, not just an administrative exercise'[14] still rings true today.

Miss Staveley fell ill at the beginning of the autumn term 1934 and died still in office in December 1934. The Sub-Warden, Miss Barry, bridged the gap and helped Dr Millicent Taylor, the newly appointed temporary Warden, run the Hall for a very short time until Miss Macleod took up the wardenship in 1935.

Jessie Winifred Macleod 1935-1965

Miss Macleod, born on 27 November 1901, obtained an MA from the University of Glasgow and a B. Litt from St Hugh College, Oxford. In 1934, she was appointed Special Lecturer in Philosophy at the University of Bristol and Warden of Clifton Hill House in August 1935.

Many students have described Miss Macleod as strict and formidable. Men were not allowed in Hall after tea-time, not even fathers or brothers! Students had to ask permission to stay out after 10.30 pm and were not always granted such a privilege, even to go to the theatre or attend a concert at the Colston Hall. As Warden, Miss Macleod acted in loco parentis and took her responsibilities very seriously.

Her strict rules gave rise to a limerick that was recently quoted on *Woman's Hour*:

> We have a Warden called Mac
> Who thinks all our morals are slack
> If we are not in by one
> She assumes our morals undone
> So we do it by ten and get back!

Ironically, Miss Macleod was accused of negligence in an article in the *News of the World* following the pregnancy of a young medical student under her care.

Like Miss Staveley, Miss Macleod was very fond of animals and was remembered for her devotion to her cat, Twinkle. However, unlike Miss Staveley, Miss Macleod was a chain-smoker, rarely seen without a cigarette.

In 1965, Miss Macleod retired from her wardenship and returned to Scotland where she died in October 1979.

Mrs Belinda Baldock 1966-1969

In her report of 1966, the Clifton Hill House Senior Student noted:

> The most notable happening this year was, of course, the change of warden. Miss Macleod left at Christmas and was presented by the students with a silver cigarette box at the carol concert following Christmas Dinner. We were without a warden during the next term, with Miss Carpenter, the Domestic Bursar taking charge temporarily. The new warden, Mrs Baldock, arrived after Easter, and seemed to settle in quickly. With the change-over the students took the opportunity to obtain a gradual relaxation of some Hall regulations, particularly those concerning the hours during which men visitors may be received in students' rooms. This is now permitted every day for all students between 4pm and 7pm and between 2pm and 10pm on Wednesdays, Saturdays and Sundays. The feared sudden invasion did not take place and the Hall quickly adapted to the greater freedom.[15]

Miss Peggy Stembridge, a colleague and friend of Mrs Baldock, had kindly written the following account of her wardenship:

Jessie Winifred Macleod.

Mrs Belinda Baldock was an able Cambridge zoologist, but after completing research in Africa she married and joined her husband, an Oxford historian, on his cattle ranch in what was still Tanganyika. After his sudden death in 1965, and managing the ranch during the country's changeover to Tanzania, she decided to return to England to work and make a home for her three children.

In 1966, Clifton Hill House was one of Bristol's two halls of residence for women students, and was currently without a Warden. In several ways, Mrs Baldock was an unconventional appointee – the first married woman, with a family, and without a continuous academic background. Aware of her apparent lack of relevant experience, she visited Wardens of Halls in some of the newer universities, so she came with a fresh outlook on student life in Hall. The interviewing committee were surprised to discover that among her varied talents she was a good rifle shot and they hoped that she would not need her hunting skills in Bristol.

CHH was steeped in over 50 years of conventions, so introducing fresh ways was not an easy task. Today's students may find it hard to believe that main Hall and the two annexes were locked at 10.30 pm and permission had to be sought at breakfast time for a late key or a weekend pass. There was an interesting social innovation: a regular reception in the JCR for students to meet senior members of the university academic staff (sometimes Nobel prize winners) and members of Senate, followed after dinner by coffee and conversation in the warden's sitting room.

Mrs Baldock could appear formidable when appropriate and was generally a rather private person, but she was a great listener, an encourager of others by word and example, and a very practical leader, with a useful sense of humour. Students were consulted and were involved as well as tutors in responsibility for events in Hall, so that a more liberal atmosphere was gradually being introduced. It was probably her capacity for innovation and practical management that inspired the Vice-Chancellor, Sir Alec Merrison, to invite her to be responsible for developing the Goldney annexe into the first self-catering hall for men and women students, a completely new model for Bristol, and to become the Warden when Goldney Hall opened in 1969. She retired from Goldney Hall in 1977. She died in 1999.

Miss Sheila Barbara Brennan, 1969-1984

Born in Liverpool in February 1905, Sheila Brennan obtained her BA from Lady Margaret Hall, Oxford, and worked at the University of Bristol as a temporary lecturer in Education between 1952 and 1955, before taking up an appointment at Fourah Bay College in Sierra Leone. After holding posts at Newton Park, Bath and at the University of Malawi, she returned to Bristol to look after her mother. She was Warden of Clifton Hill House from 1969 to 1984, and of Manor Hall from 1974 to 1984. She also served as Chairman of the Wardens' Committee and as Special Lecturer in the Education Department, where she ran many courses catering for the needs of international students. Her work as Adviser to Overseas Students between 1968 and 1987 will be remembered with gratitude by several generations who studied at the University. She was a caring warden and helped many students settle in their university career. In retirement she made a number of visits to Argentina and Paraguay to visit her nearest surviving relatives.

Miss Sheila Barbara Brennan.

Mrs Adrienne Mason.

Mrs Adrienne Mason, 1984-1988

Born in Scotland in 1945, Adrienne Mason studied French and Latin in Reading and was a postgraduate at Birkbeck College, London. She returned to Scotland in 1970 to teach at the University of Glasgow until 1982, spending a year as a lecturer in the University of Dijon from 1979-1980. After her marriage in 1982, she moved to Bristol and was appointed as Warden of Clifton Hill House in 1984 where she remained until 1988. She also taught part-time in the University of Exeter, until she was appointed to a full-time post in the University of the West of England.

She recalls:

When, in the summer of 1983, I was offered a post as Warden of Clifton Hill House, I jumped at the chance, even if I had only the haziest idea of what this august person was actually supposed to do. Alan Rump, the Warden of Churchill Hall, described the role, 'I see a warden as an enabler'. That is exactly, it seems to me, what the warden of a hall of residence should be. Every year of my brief four-year tenure reminded me how much each new generation of students valued the hall and just how much they contributed to it. Without them (and the long-suffering staff), I could not have opened the house

Mrs Annie Burnside.

to the public around an exhibition devoted to John Addington Symonds, nor would we have had the succession of concerts, plays and social events that marked each year. Most poignantly, it was during that time that the students organised and hosted the first Convivium, celebrating the life of Clement Wheeler-Bennett, who had done so much for the Hall despite the relentless progress of a terminal illness.

Mrs Mason is a prize-winning translator and has recently returned to the University of Bristol where she co-ordinates the MA in Translation.

Mrs Annie Burnside, 1988-

Born in November 1944, Annie Burnside was brought up in Paris and read English at the Sorbonne where she was awarded a D.E.S. and the C.A.P.E.S. in English Language and Literature. She obtained her MA in Classical French Literature from the University of Bristol in 1972, became language assistant in the Department of French in 1980, and Warden of Clifton Hill House in 1988. She is married to a dental surgeon and has two sons. In 1980, she founded the Ecole Française de Bristol and the Alliance Française de Bristol in 1983. She was Présidente de l'Union des Français du Sud-Ouest de Grande Bretagne from 1982 to 2004. She is 'Officier dans l'Ordre des Palmes Académiques', and 'Chevalier dans l'Ordre National du Mérite'. She has been French Honorary Consul for Bristol and the South-West of England since 2003. In 2004 she was appointed one of the two Deputy Marshals of the University. She has a special interest in student welfare, art, architecture and literature.

Notes

1 E.E. Butcher, *Clifton Hill House, the first phase*, p 5, Bristol, 1959.

2 Margaret Vaughan makes a small mistake as Callander House was, in fact, sold two years later.

3 M. Symonds (Mrs Vaughan), *Out of the Past*, op. cit., p 18.

4 E.E. Butcher, *Clifton Hill House, the first phase,* op. cit., p 5.

5 M. Symonds (Mrs Vaughan), *Out of the Past*, op. cit., p 18.

6 K. Furse, *Hearts and Pomegranates*, p 286, London, 1940.

7 J.A. Symonds bought Callander House from Joseph Haynes Nash for £3,800 on 29 September 1876. J.H. Nash had bought it from Lewis Fry of Goldney House on 30 October 1866. It had been the childhood home of Professor Sayce, the well-known Assyriologist. One famous tenant in the early 1880s was Dr John Percival, first Headmaster of Clifton College. Catherine Symonds leased Callander House for seven years to Mrs Mary Wood on 25 March 1903 at £150 p.a. The tenancy was renewed on a yearly basis. Notices were given to Mrs Mary Wood to vacate Callander House by 25 March 1916.

8 Clifton Hill House Old Students Association, *In Memoriam May C. Staveley, Clifton Hill House, 1909-1934*, Bristol, 1935.

9 E.E. Butcher, *Clifton Hill House, the first phase*, op. cit., pp 10-11.

10 Ibid., p 11.

11 Ibid., p.11.

12 Clifton Hill House Old Students' Association, *In Memoriam May C. Staveley, Clifton Hill House, 1909-1934*, op., cit., p 3.

13 E.E. Butcher, *Clifton Hill House, the first phase*, op. cit., pp 8-9.

14 E.E. Butcher, *Clifton Hill House, the first phase*, op. cit., p 18.

15 1966 Report in the CHHOSA Magazine edited by Ann Stark. See last chapter.

The magnificent Palladian staircase, restored in 2002. The walls were painted a delicate pink, the egg-and-dart and Vitruvian scroll motifs were gilded. The ceiling is a typical Isaac Ware arrangement of oval and oblong panels. The oval compartment with the fine rococo plasterwork was renovated and a lantern now hangs from the original hook. Note the elaborately scrolled wrought-iron balusters with foliage sprays and fern-leaves.

Restoring the House: 1988 to 2009

The restoration programme, with the aim of improving the facilities available to students, and to do justice to the Grade I listed buildings of Clifton Hill House, was begun by the present Warden, Mrs Annie Burnside, shortly after her appointment in 1988. Since the University had acquired the House in 1909, the Hall had gradually expanded away from the old House, leaving in its wake some fine but tired and institutionalised rooms, some less fine but large, and many partitioned rooms. It was clear that a major rolling programme would be needed to improve the décor. It is worth noting that in 1988, there was little enthusiasm for change and much scepticism about the usefulness of such an undertaking. However, one important project was completed almost every year and sometimes even two or three. All the redecoration work was designed and carried out by the Bristol interior decorator, Anthony Richards.

The first priority of the restoration programme was to address the sad and institutional interior of the original house, revitalising rooms that had lost their purpose. The next task was to improve the connecting areas between the two houses, Callander House and Clifton Hill House. The Print Gallery adjacent to the Foyer area, was a new creation designed to give life to an otherwise soulless corridor. One now moves from one room to another in a more harmonious fashion.

Redecoration – even creation – was also carried out in key areas of the 1960 Fry Wing: the entrance hall, the students' dining room, the ladies' cloakroom that was to become the Symonds Library, the Junior Common Room and the Three Horses Bar where an external staircase was built to echo the Palladian staircase and to give direct access to the Fry Garden.

There follows a selection of the work completed.

Restoration works since 1988

The Wills Reception Room 1988

The main dining room 1989

The main entrance hall 1989

The Print Gallery 1990

The main staircase 1992

The Foyer 1993

The Symonds Library 1994

The Fisher drawing room 1994

The Symonds music room 1995

The computer room 1995

The JCR and bar 1996

The Senior Common Room 1996

The external staircase to the Fry Garden 1996

The Gothic study 1997

The garden level renovation 1999/2000

The foyer: second renovation 2001

The restoration of the Palladian staircase 2002

The second redecoration of the main dining room 2002

The redesigning of the Symonds Library mezzanine 2003

The redesigning of the Wills reception room 2004/05

The redesigning of the Print Gallery 'garden' 2006/07

The re-instatement of the three window-boxes on the 1853 wing 2008

The dining room funded by Sir George Wills in 1919.

Restored as the Wills Reception Room in 1998.

The 1919 dining room. Restored in 1988, now the Wills Reception Room

In 1919, ten years after the house became the first Hall of Residence for Women at the University of Bristol, this room was built onto the site of the stable block courtyard, to provide a new dining room for the then forty resident students. It was one of the many projects funded by Sir George Wills. In 1995, the Warden named the room after him; it is thus now known as the Wills Reception Room.

In the 1960s a larger dining room was built in Fry Wing and the 1919 dining room became a reading room. It was sadly institutional until it was completely redesigned by Anthony Richards in 1988, as an eighteenth-century Adam-style reception area. A photograph taken of this room before it was redecorated shows a dismal and feature-less room. With the additions of a dado rail, plaster wall panelling, a cornice and ceiling roses the room was radically transformed. With the resurfacing of the parquet floor, and with a pair of glass chandeliers, the room could rival the original ones across the corridor. A second door was created through the back wall to give direct access to and from the Foyer.

The Wills Reception Room is now a multi-purpose room regularly used by students for parties, play rehearsals or even for revising for exams. It is also in great demand for seminars, conferences, and is licensed for wedding ceremonies and receptions.

A classical plaque where a glazed partition once stood.

The 'Works Canteen' – restored in 1989

The students' dining room was known as the 'Works Canteen'. During the redecoration work, the pilasters were painted to give a marble effect and wooden pediments were added above the windows and doors to replace the 1960s curtains.

below: The 'works canteen' before the 1989 restoration.

left and bottom: Transformed into an elegant dining room.

The Print Gallery – created in 1990

The Print Gallery was created out of an awkward corridor with 1950s glazed partitions. These were in-filled with panels and painted a soft Etruscan red.

Print rooms were fashionable between 1755 and 1820, but few have survived.

An interest in the 1990s in the decorative value of prints led to a revival of the technique and inspired this Print Gallery.

In 2006, the Gallery had to be recreated after both walls were unfortunately damaged by some badly-thought-out DDA (Disability Discrimination Act) work, when a very dominant ramp and ugly handrails were introduced. A new arrangement of prints taken mostly from Colen Campbell's *Vitruvius Britannicus* relate almost entirely to the works of Isaac Ware, the celebrated Palladian architect of Clifton Hill House.

top: The corridor before 1990.

left: Afterwards, transformed into the Print Gallery.

70

The Symonds Library – created in 1994

This room was created in 1994 from a large and little-used 1960s ladies' cloakroom in Fry Wing. Mr Michael Parry, then Registrar of the University, allocated a budget for a break-out room, especially for conference use. However, in order to give it more of an identity, the Warden conceived it as a room devoted to the Symonds family who had lived in, loved and changed Clifton Hill House in the nineteenth-century. Here all the Symonds items that were scattered around the Hall and in great danger of being forgotten or lost would be displayed. And some indeed had been lost. Bookcases from the Symonds Music Room were cut to size and installed where previously there was a row of washbasins.

The Library houses a permanent exhibition of the Symonds family memorabilia in a Victorian décor. Etruscan red walls form a strong background for the many pictures and photographs on display. The University Library Special Collections provided letters, photographs and other documents. Inspiration for the lighting was drawn from a photograph of the drawing room at Clifton Hill House in the 1870s.

The portrait of Dr Symonds shows him in his early thirties when he was elected Physician to the General Hospital and Lecturer in Forensic Medicine at the Bristol Medical School.

Of particular note within the Symonds Library is the plaster cast of the marble bust of Dr Symonds by his friend Thomas Woolner (1825-1892), the only sculptor in the Pre-Raphaelite Brotherhood, founded in 1849. Woolner spent a fortnight at Clifton Hill House in August 1865, modelling Dr Symonds's head. The marble bust was displayed at the Royal Academy in 1872. Woolner also sculpted, among others, the busts of

above: The ladies' cloakroom before the 1994 restoration and *below*: Afterwards as the Symonds Library.

Plaster cast of the bust of Dr Symonds by Thomas Woolner, executed from life in 1865 at Clifton Hill House, and given to Miss Staveley for the Hall by Henry Stratchey (Dr Symonds's grandson) in 1930.

A corner of the library where toilets once stood. Now with a marble bas-relief of Charlotte Symonds executed in the classical manner at Davos in 1892. It was given to the Hall by the Hon. Mrs Charles Leaf in 1950.

Darwin, Newman, Kingsley and Dickens.

A whole section of the Library is devoted to John Addington Symonds, the literary critic, historian and poet, son of Dr Symonds, who moved into Clifton Hill House after his father's death in 1871.

A plaster bust of Dante that had belonged to John Addington Symonds, and was on loan to the Italian Department, was kindly returned to Clifton Hill House by Professor Judith Bryce when the Symonds Library was created. The date of the bust is probably 1865, the year of the sexcentenary of Dante's birth. Dante is shown beardless as in Giotto's and Botticelli's portraits. John Addington Symonds wrote *An Introduction to the Study of Dante* at Clifton Hill House in 1872.

In 1880, the Symondses exiled themselves to Davos hoping for a cure for Symonds's lung disease. There is an interesting display of family photographs of the time when Symonds started the Winter Games at Klosters.

An area previously occupied by a row of toilets has now been replaced with more attractive items relating to the Symonds family, in particular:

The marble bas-relief of Charlotte Symonds[1] was given to the Hall in 1950 by Charlotte's daughter-in-law, the Hon Mrs Charles Leaf.

Edward Lear's 'The Owl and the Pussy Cat' was written for the Symonds's eldest daughter, Janet, as was 'The Duck and the Kangaroo', a facsimile of which is displayed. Also on display in the Symonds Library are photocopies of letters from Symonds which are testimonies of the long friendship between Edward Lear and the Symonds.

The official opening of the library took place in March 1995. An eclogue written in Cannes, in 1867, by Symonds, his wife, and Edward Lear was acted by Clifton Hill House students. A musical interlude was given by tenor Kevin McLean-Mair and pianist Graham Lloyd. They performed the première of the musical setting by contemporary English composer Ian Venables of John Addington Symonds's Venetian poetry. Since then, Ian Venables's musical compositions for Symonds's poetry have been recorded no fewer than three times and are sung by the tenor Ian Partridge.

John Vaughan and Chris Furse, both descendants of the Symonds family, reaffirmed their connection with Clifton Hill House. Since 1909, when the House was sold to the University, members of the Symonds family have kept in touch with Clifton Hill House. They have been pleased to offer to the Hall inherited family treasures that they often did not have space for in their own homes. In a letter of 30 July 1950 to Miss Macleod, Katharine Furse noted: 'We are all in the same position trying to find homes for what we cannot house ourselves.' Speaking of some fine family portraits she added: 'It seems to be a pity, in this case, where there is association, not to offer the pictures but I shall understand if they are refused.' Miss Macleod eagerly accepted the family portraits. Unfortunately, only that of Edith Cave[2] remains; it now hangs in the Symonds Library.

The Symonds Library is very popular with the Clifton Hill House students and is often hired out for small meetings.

A plaster cast of the northern frieze of the Parthenon is displayed outside the Symonds Library – the cast had previously belonged to the Symonds family. It is a fitting introduction to the library, as Symonds was himself a distinguished classicist who taught Latin and Greek at Clifton College. He also wrote *Studies of the Greek Poets*, in two volumes.

left:
Edward Lear's 'The Duck and the Kangaroo' illustrated by John Addington Symonds for Janet.

below:
Plaster cast of the northern frieze of the Parthenon.

The Fisher Drawing Room – restored in 1995

Like the Symonds Music Room next door, this room had been originally painted a nondescript magnolia colour with a harsh white paint on the ceilings.

During the restoration a copy of an eighteenth-century blue and off-white damask wallpaper was used for the walls. The classical motifs of the cornice in the Fisher Drawing Room were picked out with gold paint, and a Bohemian crystal chandelier in the eighteenth-century style was introduced to replace the heavy Teutonic lights of the 1920s. All the doors were painted to simulate mahogany wood.

left: The Fisher Drawing Room in the twenties.

below left and right:
The Fisher Drawing Room before restoration, and after.

The Symonds Music Room – restored in 1995

The Symonds Music Room still has Georgian proportions but is strongly Victorian in the design of the fireplace and the very tall windows. The same damask wallpaper as in the Fisher Drawing room brings harmony to the two rooms.

Like other restored areas of the Hall, these rooms are extensively used by students for all sorts of activities. They are also very popular for seminars, weddings and other receptions. The rooms were hired for several episodes of the BBC series *The House of Eliott* and *Casualty*. This has substantially increased the Hall's income.

Concerts are regularly performed in the Symonds Music Room where Dame Clara Butt, the Bristol-born contralto, gave a concert in 1920 to launch a fund for the equipment of the newly acquired Manor House.

above right:
The Symonds Music Room in the twenties.

right:
The Symonds Music Room after restoration.
The door is painted to simulate mahogany.

The Gothic Study – restored in 1997

The room was previously the office of the Hall/Warden Secretary; it had suffered the indignity of 1950s cupboards, an ugly glazed partition, and five of the six Gothic finials had been broken off.

Once the glazed partition had been removed, the delicate finials re-instated and the ribbed vaulting painted a subtle grey and off-white colour, the Gothic study was remarkably transformed. It is lit by spotlights and a Gothic lantern; Gothic prints by Batty Langley were used to furnish the walls.

left:
The Gothic Study before the 1997 restoration.

below:
The Gothic Study after restoration.

The Palladian staircase and east front elevation – restored and cleaned in 2002

The cleaning and the restoration of this important Palladian stone staircase took place in the spring of 2002, partly thanks to the bequest of Miss Petherick, a 1927 student of Modern History at the University and former resident of Clifton Hill House, and also thanks to a fund-raising campaign following an article by Professor Tim Mowl in the University of Bristol magazine *Nonesuch*. In addition the London Georgian Group contributed financially to the project.

The friable Bath stone of the staircase had crumbled in many places and damaged balusters had to be replaced.

The cleaning of the middle elevation and of the vermiculated rustication that had become very black over the years revealed the poor repairs carried out in the 1960s. Many of the brackets holding the stones had rusted and had to be removed. The work was more extensive than first thought. It lasted for many weeks.

In November 2004, Clifton Hill House was the winner of the London Georgian Group Architectural Award in the category 'Restoration of a Georgian Country House'. This prestigious national award is held annually to assess the best restoration works across the United Kingdom and attracted 87 entrants that year. Prince Michael of Kent presented the award at a gala evening at Christie's in Mayfair.

Damage to stonework on the staircase.

The blackened stonework of the garden side elevation before cleaning...

...and after.

Future improvement projects

Clifton Hill House, a Grade I listed building, is a gem in the crown of historical buildings owned by the University of Bristol. It is hoped that the House will continue to be well maintained. There are several further projects under consideration:

- Cleaning the nineteenth-century wings and re-instating the three window boxes on the 1853 wing according to a period photograph. This should be completed in 2009.

- Restoring the derelict south-east turret at the bottom of the garden to match the south-west turret. Both turrets pre-date the house and were probably built in the early 1700s.

- Re-instating of the Edwardian veranda built in 1914 outside the Foyer area.

- Unearthing the marble busts of Roman emperors and philosophers that were buried at the bottom of the garden by the Symonds in 1880.

- Installing en-suite pods in student study-bedrooms would meet the high demand for such essential facilities from both students and conference delegates.

The London Georgian Group Architectural Award, left to right: Alison Allden, Deputy Registrar; John MacDonald, stonemason; Annie Burnside, Warden; Anthony Richards, interior decorator.

Notes

1 Charlotte (1867-1934) was the Symondses' second daughter. The marble bas-relief was carved at Davos by the young sculptor Townsend, before her marriage in 1894 to the Greek scholar Walter Leaf. Townsend later died at Davos of tuberculosis.
2 Edith Harriette Symonds was John Addington's eldest sister. She married Sir Charles Cave who had the Old Bank, Bristol.

The tulipière

The present Warden would like to record her thanks to the committee of the CHHOSA (The Clifton Hill House Old Students Association) for presenting to her a blue and white china tulipière at the 1999 AGM in recognition of her friendship and services to the Association and to mark over ten years of restoration work in the Hall. The tulipière in Delftware style was designed by Francis Ceramics; it is decorated at the base with the view of Clifton Hill House and its grounds.

Ex-Clifton Hill House students' reminiscences of their time in Hall

This chapter has been devised with Clifton Hill House students past, present, and particularly future in mind. It offers a fascinating insight into what life was like in Hall one hundred years ago, and how it has evolved and adapted in parallel with the huge social, economic, and political changes that occurred during that time, while still retaining many of the same values. The early reminiscences were kindly edited by Ann Stark, herself a Clifton Hill House student (1961-1964) and Secretary to the CHHOSA (Clifton Hill House Old Students Association) for forty years. Her contribution has been tremendous. Ann writes:

As Secretary I have been the keeper of the CHHOSA archives. It seemed appropriate that in 2009 which is the centenary of the founding of Clifton Hill House as a Hall of Residence I should make these archives accessible to others, albeit in a limited fashion. I hope that my modest researches will in some way honour the memories of those who went before. It is not meant as a history of CHH – others more able than I have already done this. I hope that it serves as a means of giving voice to those for whom CHH meant so much. The majority of the material is of its time but in some cases I have included memoirs written many years later at the request of Mrs Burnside who expressed a great interest in the memories of 'old' students who were still alive. However, I am bound to have left out a great deal which should have been

included and for this I apologise.

If there is any merit to be extracted from my offerings, then I dedicate it in particular to the memories of Mary Williams (née Minton) and Phyllis Mattock (née Gordon) who served CHH and CHHOSA so devotedly and who became such good friends to me.

Ann Stark (née Bussey) Secretary, CHHOSA, February 2009

The CHHOSA Committee 1989-1998
left to right back row: Mary Williams sitting, Marjorie Perry, Ann Stark, Evelyn Libra, Damaris Falconer
front row: Joan Hughes, Annie Burnside, Phyllis Mattock, Sarah Nicholas.

There were 21 students in residence at the Hall last year, and five members of staff.

Part of the Gymnasium has been partitioned off temporarily to make room for 3 students. These rooms are the envy of everyone for they open onto the balcony! This makes a delightful open-air study, and four or five students have been sleeping there during the summer. The rest of the Gymnasium was used for its proper purpose during the winter. We drilled from 6 to 6.45 on Wednesdays, taking it in turn to conduct the class.

On October 28 we were fortunate enough to have a visit from Mr and Mrs John Masefield. They came to Bristol for the representation of Mr Masefield's new play 'The Armada', which was a great success.

After dinner every evening we have been very busy knitting socks and other things for sailors and soldiers. A good many things have been sent off by the University. If any old student would like to send us her work we should be very pleased to send it away with ours. It is really quite depressing to think how very little we students can do to help at such a time as this. It makes us often pause to think if we are doing the right thing to go on living in such pleasant and peaceful surroundings when so many of our friends are in such terrible trouble and distress.

Mrs Mallet has very kindly lent us a collection of water colours painted by Mr Lewis Fry. We have hung them in the Library and Common Room, and they are a great addition to the decoration of these rooms. We are to be allowed to keep three of these paintings. Two are very nice landscapes painted in rather a modern style, and one we are to choose from the collection.

There has been plenty of tennis this year, the weather having been perfect. Of course, we left the poor old court very bare! Miss Harvey and Miss Bracher won the tournament.

Our Belgian family live quite near to us and we know the children well. They love to come and play with us in the garden, and they are most friendly and nice. At Christmas we had a Christmas tree party for them, which was great fun.

Bobby still keeps the neighbourhood awake with his cheerful voice. Ginger joins us in deciding that this is the nicest house in the world to live in. Wendy, Tsu and Lu are not ordinary mortals, and we feel it a great honour if they allow us to speak to them.

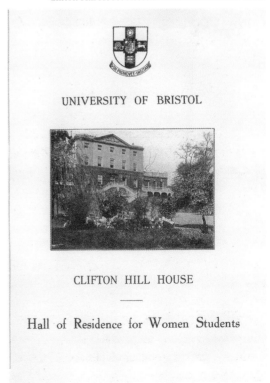

Clifton Hill House Accommodation booklet of 1914.

UNIVERSITY OF BRISTOL

CLIFTON HILL HOUSE

Hall of Residence for Women Students

The CHH tennis court disappeared under the extensions of the early 1960s.

The Belgian family were refugees and were 'adopted' by Hall.

The Warden, Miss Staveley, had a large ménagerie of pets. Bobby, the parrot, Ginger, the cat, Wendy, Tsu and Lu, the Pekinese dogs.

AN ACCOUNT OF THE VISIT BY FORMER STUDENTS IN MAY 1915, N.E. WILKINS

We did everything, and we did nothing! That means we did all the things we have done since 1909, but we did them so naturally that we hardly realised we were doing them. But there was one very pleasant innovation. The present students invited us to a supper party on Saturday evening on the balcony of the Gymnasium, which was decorated with Chinese lanterns. Someone, with much feeling, said it was quite Arabesque, but the less romantic of us were content to think it was just like the Hall. In fact, it rather reminded us of the evening when we acted 'Comus' in the garden.

Sundays are the same, too, we found. We wandered around the garden in the morning in groups, some going this way and some another, and so we had the opportunity of meeting everyone. We had tea in the garden in the shady spot between the mulberry tree and the copper beech. Miss Staveley came too, and so did the little dogs – there are three of them now – and Ginger. Ginger is the cat who took up his abode at the Hall two or three years ago. He hasn't taken the place of Charles Edward, who has now become old and staid, and has nothing to do with the students, but lives in the kitchen. Everyone wanted to go to Leigh Woods Church in the evening. It sounds alarming but we were only five.

Whit Monday was a lovely day, and we had a delightful picnic. We went to New Passage and had lunch by the Severn, and afterwards walked on to Aust, where we paddled in the mud. We had meant to be back early, but it was so very hot that we spent the whole day there.

Monday was for pleasure; Tuesday was for work. Mr Lewis Fry junior has lent the Hall a collection of his paintings, and we hung them on Tuesday morning in the common room and library. As a reward for our labour we had coffee in Miss Staveley's room.

We spent all the odd moments in visiting different students, searching for snails among the irises, playing tennis, watering the sweet peas, watching the dogs, and keeping a sharp lookout for Ginger, who prowled around looking for young birds.

It is really quite impossible to describe what we did at Whitsuntide. Everything is just the same; the goldfish are still happy in the pond; Bobby still screeches when we want him to be quiet; we still stand under the ilex and wonder when we shall be able to walk in Callendar House garden, and we still for the sixth summer, criticise the tomatoes in the greenhouse, and say they are too far behind for the time of year.

It was for many years the custom of former students to return to Hall for the Whitsuntide holiday and to join in the activities of current students. This undoubtedly enhanced the feeling of 'family' and community spirit which has always been part of the ethos of CHH.

New Passage was a popular place to visit as it was the ferry crossing embarkation point to South Wales before the building of the Severn Bridges.

Miss Staveley's visit to Donremy in August 1915

In 1915 Miss Staveley, Warden of CHH, visited Donremy in France. It was, of course, during the time of the Great War and although the village looked much the same as in the time of Jeanne D'Arc some five hundred years before, then all was not as peaceful as it might have seemed. 'Always,' she commented, 'like dread thunder, was heard the relentless, insistent roar of the guns from over the hills where the tragic drama is unfolding itself.'

She goes on to describe Sunday in this part of France which in many ways war and the passing of time had not touched and then writes of her visit to the little cottage where Joan and her family had lived. However, in the nearby church, empty of sight-seers except for Miss Staveley herself, were 'soldiers, who are now seen in every church in France kneeling to implore the help that had saved la Patrie 500 years before.'

Miss Staveley was later to speak over breakfast to a shy young soldier who spoke of the horrors of the war and of France's inadequate preparations for the first rush of the 'Boches' which had killed so many of his class mates. He had added, almost to himself, 'If England had not been with us, the war would now be over, and France would have been destroyed, but together!' She noted that the pause was more eloquent than words – and from the distance still came the sullen roar of the big guns.

Excerpts from the Senior Student's Report 1916

Many of us have come to an end of our stay at the Hall this year. It is with mixed feelings of pleasure and regret that we do so – pleasure at the thought of beginning our new work, and regret for all the pleasant days we have spent together in such delightful surroundings. There were sixteen students in residence this year, and four

Miss Staveley holding the hand of the young Belgian boy.

members of staff.

The war still casts a shadow over all our doings at the Hall as well as in College, and though our reading goes on very much as before, there is little news of interest to record. Little interest has been shown for dancing on Saturday evenings. Making warm quilts for French refugees was more to our taste – an occupation out of which we managed to derive a great deal of fun. We knitted diligently on other evenings, and altogether we have turned out a considerable number of warm wraps of one kind or another.

Our Belgian guests are still with us...the two elder girls have been at school in London this year, but the other six children know us well and are never tired of playing with us in the garden. One Sunday they had a tea party in the figgery and issued invitations. We dressed up in grand clothes for the occasion and behaved very properly!

On June 22 Miss Staveley was 'At Home' to women students. We intended to spend the evening in the garden, but it turned out so wet that we had to amuse ourselves indoors with dancing and charades.

Ginger still keeps well and happy, in spite of rather severe treatment in spring on account of his undue love for young birds; also the little dogs, in spite of much spoiling. Tsu has developed a wonderful singing voice which vies even with that of Bobbie in richness and tone!

Grace M. Hadley

One former student, Miss M. Lewis writes of her experiences doing 'Canteen Work' for the YMCA at an army camp on Salisbury Plain. She speaks of the links wrought with the young men in training for the trenches of Normandy, and of the inevitable day when 'the division moves out to France, to make way for another, and you watch them march away, still joking and singing and later they write to you from their muddy ruts to tell you how the boys are still going strong but some have gone under.'

1917-18 (EDITED BY ANN STARK)

The Clifton Hill House Old Students Association continued to grow with everyone anxious to keep in touch with old friends and the 'goings-on' in Hall itself. Many former students returned to visit during the year. Life Membership subscriptions had flowed in and allowed for a bursary fund to be set up from which £5 was immediately granted. The Senior Students (there were two during the academic year) continued to write of domestic events in their reports which emphasised the feeling of a 'continuing family life' which formed a great part of CHH's ethos. 'One feels convinced that no Hall of Residence can be complete unless it contains, as ours does, both a baby and a goat!' wrote Miss Searle in May 1918. Jane, the goat, was walked from Temple Meads protesting loudly, all the way up Park Street to Hall. The goat was established in a little house (freshly whitewashed) at the bottom of the garden and became quite content as 'There were a great many people whose main object in life seemed to be to gather for her delicacies in the shape of crunchy chestnuts, laurel leaves and ivy.'

She continues, 'The garden has given us great scope for our labours this year, as we are unable to get a gardener. By taking turns to do a little each day, we were able to maintain a general cared-for aspect on the lawn and terrace, but I am afraid the remoter corners would not bear inspection! We grew quite a number of potatoes, using a patch in Callander gardens as well.' The birth of a kid to Jane was noted which had to be rescued on several occasions from very precarious positions on the stonework of the terrace.

Ever mindful of the care of her girls, Miss Staveley had, earlier in the year in February, rented a little Mendip cottage which she allowed them to use at weekends.

More interest arose in May with the alterations in Callander House and the arrival of furniture, acquired by the very arduous labours of Miss Staveley and her deputy, Miss Barry.

Entertainments seem modest compared with the expectations of modern students, but were thoroughly enjoyed. There was a garden performance of *Twelfth Night* (which was later repeated to raise money for the University Belgian Hostel), a Freshers' entertainment which included a sketch entitled 'Mr Punch's Potted Films' and an evening picnic in the moonlight at Failand. There was a Christmas Children's Fair where students dressed up as circus animals and raised funds for the Belgian Hostel.

Old students wrote of their war work. Miss Hilda Keen wrote from France where she was on active service with

The British Expeditionary Force. Her job was to teach folk dancing, i.e. country, morris and sword dancing to the soldiers. It meant a lot of travelling to remote camps but attracted between 300-400 men and perhaps 30-40 dancers all squeezed into one hut.

Miss Jago told of a YMCA Concert Party where after a series of minor disasters the show still went on and 400 hundred soldiers were left 'cheery and happy' as a result of their efforts.

Sadly, there were deaths for which condolences were offered. One former student lost her elder brother and her younger brother was badly crippled. She herself spent every spare moment engaged in war work.

Other former students were congratulated on their forthcoming marriages. One fiancé, however, was fighting in northern France and no wedding date could be fixed.

The war, of course, could never be ignored even within the delightful confines of CHH. In the spring Miss Searle reported that 'Another feature of the term was margarine queues! Several mornings, students rose early and stood before breakfast outside a certain little shop on Blackboy Hill, where a small quantity of margarine was sold to each. What a joy it was, after the long wait, to march off proudly with one's little parcel, and to jeer at certain bed-loving friends who were still standing at the end of a long line of people. The spoils with which they returned were welcomed by Mrs Owen, who was finding the shopping a great difficulty.'

Intellectual pursuits continued. In the spring students were introduced to the poetical works of Sir Rabindranath Tagore by Professor Leonard who had met the great poet. Miss Clare Phillips (later to be one of CHHOSA's several centenarians) wrote amusingly of a Geography Course in Aberystwyth which, after several intense lectures, culminated in her having her skull scrutinised to see if she was 'Alpine-Nordic or pure Nordic.'

1918-1919

Editor's note: As I have delved into the CHHOSA archives I have been continually impressed by the idea of 'family' and a pride of having lived in CHH that permeates the reports of the day and the letters of former students. The Secretary of CHHOSA, Miss Hadley, records that many former students had written to say that it would be nice to have a Clifton Hill House in every town. 'Even the nicest hostel for mistresses does not quite satisfy them, and we all realize sooner or later that Clifton Hill House is ideal and that it is useless to cry out for the moon,' she concludes.

One correspondent, Miss Casson, went as far as putting her feelings into verse. The following is just a portion of 133 lines!

It was a bright October afternoon
When first I saw the Hall. Its great front door
Suggested nothing of that fairyland
It shows when it is opened, and one sees
The garden down below. I had not read
What Symonds wrote of it. How often since
I have felt glad to open wide that door
That strangers who were passing might enjoy
The view of tree tops glowing in the sun
Seen through the cool dark shadow of the Hall.

As always there were continual visits by old students anxious to maintain their links with Hall. If they could not visit then they wrote of their work and other exploits. Miss Odling, a science teacher in London, wrote of her previous war work in 1917 as a 'principal overlooker' in the Cannon Cartridge Cordite Filling Factory in Woolwich Arsenal. The work was both dangerous and tiring but she had been sorry to leave. Prior to that she had worked in YMCA huts. She wrote that 'The men were ridiculously grateful for any little thing one did for them.' Living in London then she was privy to the end-of-war celebrations noting that 'The Armistice and Peace celebrations have been quite wonderful. The crowds have usually been quite, if not more, interesting than the actual processions.' The following year she was able to visit her sister in Switzerland. Post-war fiscal problems made for difficulties crossing France. Only 1,000 francs per person was allowed to cross the frontier and she was fortunate not to be stripped and searched as had happened to many others.

Miss Elizabeth Butcher pointed out in her letter that Staffordshire, where she now worked as a peripatetic instructress of pupil teachers, consisted of more than just a simple division between the Potteries and the Black Country. Indeed, her work led her into very rural areas and her modes of travel sometimes proved unusual. On one occasion she travelled in an open trolley car along a rail used for limestone transportation to reach a school. She remarked upon the kindness of the welcome that she usually received in such schools, observing that it was probably due to 'the scarcity of visitors in rural districts, and the dearth of congenial society for the head teachers.' Miss M. Phillips also liked her teaching job but found her surroundings depressing. 'I find the 'Lancashire lass' most charming and responsive' she wrote. 'But Bolton itself is a terrible place, and I don't suppose I shall be able to stand it for many years. It lives in medieval filth by medieval standards, and every blade of grass in the place has been stamped out to make room for cotton. How I pine for the South!'

By now the 'adopted' Belgian family had returned to Brussels. A letter from one of the children to her friends back in Bristol would no doubt prove of interest to modern social historians and followers of fashion. She tells of her sister Maria who 'has now got her hair up since last month. I don't think she looks at all bad. I even prefer her like that because she looks more grown up.' She then enquires 'I wonder how you are getting on and I do hope you don't have difficulties with servants. Here in Belgium they are very troublesome – they want fearfully high wages and if you don't let them do exactly what they like they just leave you and go somewhere else.'

Hall itself continued to expand. In 1918 Callander House opened, providing a further seventeen study-bedrooms, all resplendent with white paint and new carpets. The Senior Student, Miss Victoria Tryon (whom many will remember because of her long attachment to CHH as student doctor) describes other changes. 'The Common Room, which was originally the kitchen of the house, is most attractive with its superior parquet floor and the French windows which lead out into the gardens.'

Even these additions could not contain all who wished to be in residence. Numbers had now swelled to forty-five and plans were already afoot to accommodate more in Manor House during the following year. Callander itself was extended with a new wing over the Gymnasium to provide eight more study-bedrooms and several bathrooms. A new dining room started to take shape in the yard between CHH and Callander which posed a perilous passage for those wishing to cross from one house to another. Miss Tryon comments, 'Altogether, we are very proud of our Hall of Residence and are always pleased to have an opportunity of showing it off to our visitors.'

However, even the charmed life of those fortunate to live in Hall in late 1918 was not enough to prevent an outbreak of influenza, although perhaps it was not recognised at that point how devastating this was to be for so many others worldwide. Following the Degree Day festivities 'Hall was attacked most savagely by that all too common disease, influenza, and many in our midst were unfortunate enough to become victims to a mild form of it and had to spend weary days upstairs, waited upon almost hourly by Miss Barry, to whom doubtless, the days must have been distinctly weary.'

Happily by spring the outbreak was over and the usual social activities recommenced. Dancing after dinner until 8pm had been the norm during the winter, mainly as a means of economising on coal. This had proved so much fun that in the spring a dancing class was started which had an attendance of 30 people. There were summer parties in the garden, a tennis tournament and an evening supper party led by Miss Staveley to Leigh Woods which culminated in 'brain wracking games' which caused considerable mirth. Other outdoor pursuits included the tending of various plots in the Callander flower borders by several enthusiastic students.

1919-20 DAME CLARA BUTT AND HALL EXTENSIONS

In February 1920 Miss Staveley invited a large number of people to CHH to meet Dame Clara Butt who had been asked for her help in fundraising to provide more student accommodation for women. Miss Hadley, writing in the CHHOSA newsletter, recorded that 'Dame Clara was greeted with great applause. She said that when she read Miss Staveley's letter telling her of the great and urgent need of room at the University Hall of Residence, and asking for help, it was with a thrill of joy that she took it up, thinking that this would be a practical way in which she might show her gratitude to Bristol. She said how she loved Bristol as her native place: here she had discovered her voice and received her early training, and here she was married. Bristol was the springboard which helped her to success, and she welcomed this opportunity of helping to make a springboard in the city she loved for other women. It was with these feelings of gratitude and appreciation that she had decided to set about the task of raising the necessary £25,000 for the much needed new wing.'

Dame Clara outlined her plans which included a concert in the Colston Hall. Miss Hadley added her own voice to the appeal at the meeting giving 'some idea of the appreciation of old students of the Hall and of Miss Staveley's work in connection with it.'

Many old students rallied to the cause although as Miss Hadley added, 'The idea of any alterations to the Hall as we knew it is naturally met with great apprehension. It was perfect as it was, and there is always a fear that it might be spoiled. But if it means making our own very happy experiences possible for more students we must become reconciled at once, and even enthusiastic for change.'

Money flowed in from former students. Although the names of their writers are unknown the following extracts from their letters speak with the one voice – that of wishing to help.

I enclose a cheque for five pounds. I never wrote one gladlier.[sic] The chance of joining in has added a spice to life these last two days.

I send my contribution to you with great gladness, for

love of Miss Staveley. I'm always thinking of her and the trouble I gave her in return for all her goodness.

My wish is to be able to send at least ten times the amount.

I hope to be able to pay back in the future as much as ever can be paid as such a debt as the one I owe Miss Staveley and the Hall.

Isn't it good of Clara Butt to give a concert to the Fund?

I think all students look back to this life in College Hall with something of gratitude, to say nothing of more intimate feelings, and I have always felt that Bristol students have good reason to be very proud of Clifton Hill House, for it compares very favourably with other University Halls. I am glad to be able to help a little towards the additional wing. At the same time, I don't think that the huge CHH of the future will be quite as enjoyable as the small one of 1914-15. What do you think?

I think it is an excellent idea to show our appreciation in this way. I shall be delighted to help.

What a tremendous place the Hall will be! But I don't think it will be a bit nicer than when we were a tiny community, so proud of our wet paint.

The ongoing changes in Hall produced some worry to both current students and to Miss Staveley and her staff. The alterations to Manor House were not finished in time for the start of the academic year but students were nevertheless found a corner in CHH. Nor was the new dining room completed on time. A strike made it impossible to get the necessary materials but eventually all was finished. The event was celebrated with a dinner party to which members of the Hall Committee and several former students were invited.

The new residents of Manor House were obviously so delighted by their new abode that they composed a song in its honour sung to the tune of 'Vive la Compagnie' and performed it on 4 June.

The Senior Student, Miss Chrystal Cates begins her annual letter by saying, 'The inhabitants of Clifton Hill might well be pardoned should they become alarmed at the continual expansion of the borders of the Hall.' However, she concludes, 'In spite of its perpetual growth, the Hall changes so little in general appearance that, however many times we visit it later, it always seems the same place.'

Any changes certainly did not put off returners to Hall. Whitsuntide saw the visit of a record number of 17 old students. The weather was fine which allowed for a tennis tournament which by now had become somewhat of a tradition.

If they could not come in person they wrote. Many described the schools in which they now taught. Miss Fraser wrote from Jamaica where tropical rains arriving unexpectedly could cancel outdoor activities by their sheer force. Miss Emery writing from Leicester sums up what several others thought of their new life. 'Teaching is intensely interesting – one learns more than one teaches – though it is often difficult and sometimes harassing. I do feel that it is one of the best of all professions.'

Miss N. Searle wrote to describe a first winter ski-ing holiday with her friend Miss Casson and family.

One puts what may be described as a thin toboggan, about six feet long, on each foot, grasps a formidable stick in each hand, and then optimistically hopes to slide to the bottom of the slope.

This account was accompanied by the first photographs to be printed in the CHHOSA newsletter and indeed, by modern standards the skis do seem to be very unwieldy! Miss Searle also included a description of her work which was:

research on model aeroplanes in the wind channels. We put them in an artificial wind, and obtain measurements, from which one can predict the degree of stability, efficiency etc. of the full scale machine.

1921-22

Lack of money did not allow for a newsletter 1920-21. To try to balance the finances it became necessary for CHHOSA to raise its subscription. The next edition thus showed a bumper crop of letters from former students anxious to tell others of their jobs, homes and trips abroad.

This dispersal of news was a two-way enterprise. Former students longed to hear of the current 'goings-on' in Hall and looked forward to the Senior Student's report. In their turn, those in residence happily welcomed former students back to Hall, particularly at Whitsuntide, and the feeling of 'family' continued undiminished.

By 1921 the numbers in Hall had increased yet again. Following the hospitality offered to former students during the Degree Day ceremonies Miss Butler (Senior Student) wrote in her report that 'Miss Staveley had evidently not grown accustomed to the swollen numbers

Manor House in the twenties.

of her flock, for she was patiently waiting for all the visitors to depart some time after the last had gone. It was some time before the startling truth dawned upon her that the crowds still left belonged to the Hall.'

Fortunately the new dining room had at long last been completed, but it now took on an additional use in the evenings as a communal study owing to a coal strike. All the students (who would normally study in their own rooms) had opted to send their meagre rations of fuel to the kitchen for cooking use or for the heating of water. Miss Staveley arranged for cocoa to be sent up at 10pm and Miss Butler records that 'the last ten minutes were spent by most of the would-be students in examining their watches and wondering if the church clock was fast or slow that day! Directly ten o'clock struck, two or three thirsty ones would rush off to Callander House kitchen to find Harriett and the two big jugs of cocoa.'

An important event was the follow-up to the earlier visit of Dame Clara Butt. She had noticed the absence of a gramophone and a few days later a gramophone and several dance records arrived in Hall for the use of the students. Her accompanying letter was proudly exhibited on the notice board. In it she compared the students to the carnations in the bouquet which they had given her. It was a cause of great grief to them on reflection as the carnations in question had been a dark red colour and not the more flattering blush pink!

Another visit was made by John Masefield who was in Bristol to see a production of his play *Tragedy of Nan*. Sadly another famous visitor to Bristol was not able to find time to call in at CHH. This was the Prince of Wales who missed the Union Flag which was displayed 'at great risk to life and limb' by the students.

The academic life of Hall was punctuated by the now traditional tea parties, dances and plays. One event worth mentioning, however, was the auction-sale party given by those about to leave. Marvellous bargains were obtained by the students who would be returning in the autumn. Miss Butler describes 'Miss Loveday's wonderful box which contained almost everything from a silver watch to a bottle of hair-oil.' Many of the goods could not be sold with 'immediate possession' as obviously no student could be expected to live – even for her last few days at the Hall – without her kettle. However, the purchasers were very kind and agreed to wait for their goods.

PHYLLIS MATTOCK (NÉE GORDON) 1926-1929

One sunny morning in 1926 a nervous and anxious young Anglo-Indian girl knocked at the front door of Clifton Hill House. The door was immediately opened by the Grande Dame herself, Miss Staveley, that tall and majestic Edwardian lady, her head crowned by gorgeous titian coloured hair. No! On this occasion she was not holding her Pekinese or King Charles spaniel. Tall and majestic lady she certainly was, but never-the-less very human and

Phyllis Mattock and Mary Williams in 1926.

understanding. She immediately called Connie Hughes and introduced me (Phyllis Gordon) to lovely and understanding Connie with whom I was to share a room for the next three years.

Those glorious three years were some of the happiest in my life. First we shared a room in Callander, but were then moved to Manor House to make room for two other students so that Miss Rhoda Barry (the sub-warden) could more closely keep her eye on them as they had been known to climb walls at night to meet the boys!

So now Manor House was our abode for the year! We had a lovely large room (now, I believe, three smaller rooms) with glass doors opening onto the lawns. On the Green (the lawned area) we lazed away that lovely summer of 1927 – either revising for exams or surreptitiously reading *Testament of Youth* by Vera Brittain, the book of the year. One incident was the unexpected glimpse of Mair Minton having a bath – also enjoyed by the window-cleaner!

The next year Connie and I moved into a large room on the top floor of Clifton Hill House. (I often pass the window – this brings back many, many memories.) Most of our year were already housed here. The best remembered incidents were our loud and noisy coffee parties where we indulged in coffee and sticky buns when we could afford them. There were no lifts or central heating in those days. Maids carried coal and water up all those flights of stairs and dirty water and ashes down.

The great events of our first year were the Freshers' play and the CHH Students' Dance. I arrived too late to take part in the play, but I was allowed to lend my best pink dance dress and pearls to the leading lady, Betty Owen. Our group consisted of a very unsophisticated lot of country bumpkins. On the occasion of The Clifton Hill Ball we could only just raise enough partners for the occasion.

In 1926 we had to ask permission to invite even our brothers into our rooms. All guests were expected to be entertained in the Library.

After three wonderful, unforgettable years I had to leave CHH when my sister arrived from India.

CLIFTON HILL HOUSE 21ST BIRTHDAY CELEBRATIONS
1 NOVEMBER, 1930

The old students began to arrive on Friday, 31 October and were coming and going in a fairly continuous stream during the whole weekend up to Tuesday morning, when the last of them left very reluctantly. There were over 90 people at the dinner on Saturday. Miss Staveley presided and the following were our guests: The Vice Chancellor and Mrs Loveday, Mrs Abbott, Mrs Mallet, Professor and Mrs Field, Mrs Burrow Hill, Dr Fawcett, Miss Worsley, Professor Leonard, Professor and Mrs Hasse, Professor and Mrs Crofts, Professor and Mrs Dobson, Professor and Mrs Reynolds, Professor and Mrs Andrew Robertson, Mr Stanley Baldock and Miss Birkhead. There were about 60 old students, representing all the years the Hall has been open, and seven present students. Other present students came in after dinner to hear the speeches.

It was a thrill to sit down to dinner with all those people surrounded by one's old friends – and an added pleasure to see Harriet enjoying it all, while helping to serve.

After the dinner came the speeches. The usual toast of the King having been given by the President, the toast of the Hall was proposed by Miss Grace Hadley, Secretary of CHHOSA.

Miss Hadley's Address:

I rise to propose the toast of Clifton Hill House, a place so very dear to the hearts of all of us here tonight. It is difficult to realize that when Miss Staveley opened this Hall in 1909, many of the students now in residence were not yet born! This thought makes us old-stagers feel our advancing years.

The House itself has an interesting history, and is in itself a fitting place for a Students' Hall of Residence, for great men have said great things within its walls. I think that a house takes on the character of those who have lived in it and their spirits haunt its rooms and passages. What could be more fitting than to have the spirits of such a family as that of John Addington Symonds haunting a Hall of Residence for students? One can imagine the house in those early days of 1909, with its little band of prim and proper students in their long dresses – and long hair, of course! As early as 1913, however, we had broken loose somewhat, and there was a rumour that some of our number had been seen in University Road throwing snowballs so that one of our learned professors was obliged to deviate from his accustomed path so as not to encounter such a sad spectacle – and one of us (low be it spoken) did return home with a black eye.

Then came the war with all the troubles and disturbances that followed in its train and after the war the great rush of students to the University, so that Clifton Hill House had to be enlarged and added to, until it reached its present size.

And now, though we have left behind the immediate influence of Clifton Hill House, we are still part of it, and we are striving to carry out its ideals and make its influence felt in other parts of England and the world. Our Old Students' Association is a great help to us in keeping alive this inspiration. It is an Association full of enthusiasm, fed by a deep-rooted affection for the Hall, which nothing could ever remove.

Of course, all Clifton Hill House students are very wonderful people. You only have to live here for a year or two, and the magic wand descends upon you and forces you to do things you would never have attempted otherwise.

A professor of this University once said, 'All Miss Staveley's geese are swans.' I think this is partly her secret of success. After all, people usually try to live up to what is expected of them, and they try to be less goose-like if their 'gooseishness' is not accepted or tolerated.

Many of our old students are filling important positions in schools and colleges in this country and in the Colonies. Many are filling the still more important positions of wives and mothers. Miss Staveley has now over 50 'grandchildren'! Not all of them are girls, but we hope that in less than 21 more years many of the girls will be in residence in their mother's rooms.

When you go into the homes that old students have made for themselves, there is often the flavour of Clifton Hill House about the furnishings and atmosphere of the place that is very attractive. The happiness and general well-being of any household depends upon its order, comfort, regularity, cheerfulness, good taste and pleasant conversation, all of which we learned to value during our residence at Clifton Hill House.

Miss Hadley then advanced to the high table and handed a cheque to Miss Staveley, saying:

On this great occasion, the 21st birthday celebrations of our Hall, we were anxious to show our gratitude for all that the Hall has meant to us in some tangible form. I have, therefore, much pleasure in handing you, Miss Staveley, on behalf of the old students, this cheque for £60, which we would like you to spend for the Hall in any way you think best.

109 old students have contributed to this gift, and there are among them members of the Hall from all the years since its beginning.

Dr Casson then rose to propose the toast of Miss Staveley. She spoke of the wonderful affection of all past students of the Hall for Miss Staveley. She recalled Miss Staveley's warm sympathy and keen personal interest in all the hopes and disappointments of her students, both when they were in college and long after they had left. She said that old students felt the greatest esteem and affection for Miss Staveley personally, and were delighted to have an opportunity of expressing it.

(Prolonged applause and 'For she's a jolly good fellow.')
On behalf of the Old Students' Association Dr Casson presented Miss Staveley with a gold wristlet watch, and a book of signatures. The book is entirely hand made. The leather cover was designed and worked by Miss Ethel Atkinson, four beautiful sepia drawings of Clifton Hill House, Callander House, Clifton Hill House gardens and the University Tower were contributed by Mrs Hill (Enid Rich), and the illustrations and printing by Miss Grace Hadley. Inside the book the words printed were:

Presented to
Miss M. C. Staveley Warden of Clifton Hill House
From its Opening as a Hall of Residence in 1909
On this occasion of its Twenty-first Birthday
Celebrations November 1, 1930
By the Members Of the Clifton Hill House
Old Students' Association In Appreciation of
Her Unceasing Devotion to the Interests of
Her Students Her Wise Guidance and Her
Warm Heart As a Token of Esteem, Gratitude
and Love.

Miss Staveley, in thanking the members of the Old Students' Association for their gifts to the Hall and to herself, referred to the generosity shown by old students to the Hall on many occasions.

They had given a number of books to the library, had contributed a large part of the cost of the tennis courts in Callander House garden, had founded bursaries, and sent many other gifts to the Hall. She hoped to confer with the old students at their next meeting as to the best way of spending this very substantial new gift.

Her 21 years of wardenship were full of happy memories. Old students showed very great affection for their Hall and visited it constantly. She was always delighted to welcome them and to keep in touch with them.

Having expressed her appreciation of the presence of so many old friends, friends who had done so much at the beginning to make the Hall possible, she said how one realized the gaps that time had inevitably made. Among these were Mr Lewis Fry, in whose house the first meeting to discuss the Hall was held, and who had always been our most encouraging and generous friend; Mr Worsley, who had given us his help and approval; the anonymous benefactor, without whom the Hall could not have been bought; and then later Sir George Wills, who with his true kindness had consented to be Treasurer; Sir Isambard and Lady Owen, and others.

After hearing the kind things that had been said about herself, she could realize the feelings of anyone who might return to this world and read the much too flattering epitaphs that had been engraved upon their tombs.

Referring to her personal gifts, Miss Staveley said how much she would treasure them – the book, expressing, as it did, much kind thought, and the watch, too, for 'Now,' she added laughingly, 'at last I shall know the time!'

She concluded by saying what a real pleasure it was to her to see so many old students meeting together in their Hall. Miss Barry was then toasted by Dr Rose Bracher. In an amusing short speech, Dr Bracher spoke of the great interest Miss Barry took in all student activities, how she encouraged them in their artistic efforts, and how she had, in the past, chosen their furniture and advised them when ill.

On behalf of the Old Students' Association Dr Bracher then presented Miss Barry with a crystal and pewter bulb bowl which had been beautifully designed and executed by Miss Roxbee.

After dinner there was a short interval, when we all had an opportunity to talk to one another, and were very pleased to welcome Mrs Leonard who had not been able to come earlier.

Three episodes from the story of the Hall were acted by old students in the gymnasium:

Episode I – 1747, Mr Paul Fisher plans with difficulty the building of Clifton Hill House
Scene – Paul Fisher's Office
This episode was written by Miss G. Hart

Episode II – 1880, John Addington Symonds bids farewell to Clifton Hill House
Scene – The Garden of Clifton Hill House
This episode was written by Professor Leonard

Episode III – 1909-1930 The Inheritors
Scene – A Study Bedroom at Clifton Hill House
This episode was written by Dr Elsie Casson.

This true story of Clifton Hill House made a very appropriate ending to our evening's celebrations – and was greatly enjoyed by everyone.

As the second Episode has been taken from actual records, and will become a serious piece of permanent history for anyone interested in Clifton Hill House, Professor Leonard wants to revise it somewhat before it is actually printed.

JANET HALL (NÉE YOUNG), 1932-1937
Some of the things I remember:
Maude's extraordinarily creamy rice puddings served regularly with other sweets at lunch – just right after a walk down to the labs and back again after three hours practical work.

'Parlour Tricks' in the elegant library after dinner about once a month, in which I often played violin solos.

Orchestra in the University Tower, and the long climb up the spiral staircase if one was too late for the lift.

Dancing in the 'gym' after dinner with Miss Staveley who sometimes joined in, and certainly encouraging us to keep going – 'Go on with your dancing. Go on with your prancing' – in the middle of a raid from the men's hostels. No man inhabited CHH in my day!

Sitting at Miss Barry's table at dinner where a lot of students' activities were collected, as the result of questions ending in 'Did you say?' Happy days and happy goings-on.

LADY JOANNA HILTON (NÉE STOTT) 1932-1935
My room was actually in Manor House which I now believe belongs to Manor Hall which was then very new. I was lucky in that my room faced south and onto the lovely Paulownia tree (I hope it is still there). We had open fires in our rooms then, with a meagre ration of coal which I remember saving and storing in the bottom drawer of my chest of drawers so as to have a really good blaze at the weekends! I think I was there in 1932 to 35 so rationing was not due to the war – just frugality. No visitors in rooms I remember – certainly not anything male! I now have a granddaughter up at Oxford, and the difference!

BARBARA WOOLWAY 1930S

I look back with pleasure to the days of living on the top floor of Callander House. There was always good company around... There was the joy of stoking up the fire in my room, making it a cosy den for talk or work, or getting dressed for a dance. One can laugh now at how we paid for the position of our rooms in fire drill – which meant jumping off backwards off a top-floor window sill in harness to abseil to the ground.

JO HANDFORD (NÉE RINGROSE) 1937-1941

The thing I recall about CHH is that bathroom at the end of the top floor, but I am unwilling to elucidate! Do you remember how many of us crammed into that very small place daily? One would be in the bath, one washing hair, someone ironing with someone else waiting to iron next, someone on the loo and I'm sure somebody boiling a kettle to fill a hot water bottle. Really, it sounds so squalid now, but it was definitely a one-off experience, wasn't it?

EVELYN LIBRA 1942 CHH IN WARTIME

The worst of The Blitz was over when I came up in 1942. The Great Hall was a shell. The city centre from Wine Street and Broadmead to the river was devastated. Here and there, throughout the city, gaps showed where individual buildings or blocks had been burned by incendiaries. But the Halls of Residence – Wills, Manor and Clifton Hill House were intact. Between them, CHH itself, with Callander and Manor House, sheltered 80 women students and two male student fire watchers.

There was, of course, a staff shortage for many had been called up to the forces, but Maud and Dorothy, the maids, Miss Garrett the portress, and Smart the houseman were still there. But the shortage meant that the students had to fend for themselves a great deal more. We shared fires, one on alternate days between pairs of rooms. Muriel and I shared in our first year and had a fire every day. We learned how to make a fire out of a minimum of coal and wood, the wood being supplemented by newspaper tightly twisted into rolls. Even then we had to be fairly economical since newspapers were meagre compared with the present day 30-40 page affairs. The skill remained well into peacetime though, until gradually in later life, central heating took over. I wonder if I could do it now? The ashes were cleared away for us next morning, though.

For most of us Hall meals were adequate, considering the rationing system, but healthy young appetites ensured that there was very little left in the dishes when we had finished. We had a rota to do duty down in the kitchen after dinner, putting the cutlery and crockery into the great cumbersome dishwasher of the time, and anything uneaten by us went into the pig bin for the war effort. At the weekend, portions of rationed foodstuffs – butter, jam etc. were put out in individual portions on the sideboard in the dining room for each of us to take away and have tea in our own rooms or entertain friends, supplemented, of course, by occasional goodies from home. Milk, thankfully, was not rationed, and we got extra supplies from the corner shop in York Place. Tea was rationed, but not coffee, and this was in the early days of Nescafé when it came in powder form in a small tin. Baths were restricted to three a week, five inches deep, and a broad red stripe was painted inside the bath so we knew when to stop running the water.

Events like the Freshers' entertainment and Hall Ball continued, and outside Hall we went to the Union dances and other student entertainments in the Victoria Rooms, in our prettiest dresses, but stocking less – stockings were on coupons. Alcohol and cigarettes were in short supply. Does anyone else remember those dreadful 'perfumed' cigarettes we smoked for lack of anything better? There was then, of course, no talk of the effect of smoking on health. We queued for the cinema, and went to concerts at the Colston Hall until it suffered in a fire, when the concerts were transferred to the Methodist Hall in Old Market. I remember John Barbirolli and the Hallé coming to play Tchaikovsky, with the glorious voice of Elizabeth Schumann singing Mozart and Pouishnoff playing Chopin. The Theatre Royal re-opened during this time too, with gallery seats at 1/6-, standing 1/-. Ballet was 2/6 and there, and at the Hippodrome, we saw the great companies and famous and future stars – my copy of *Twelfth Night* still has the cast pencilled in with Patrick Troughton as Sebastian.

There was still the occasional raid, however, and students of twenty and over served as fire watchers. Those under twenty could volunteer, and after one night in the basement of CHH during a raid I volunteered – how I hated that feeling of being shut in underground. My post was in the Wills Building, and the command post was on the ground floor where the Department of Geology now is. There was a two-hour watch in a 'tin tabernacle' on the floor of the tower, directly beneath Great George, who, of course, was silent during those years. The pigeons roosted there and from time to time the pigeon catchers came in to collect them. The bell was in what one can only call 'a right state' from their droppings. The post was a useful 'hostel' too. In August 1944 I bagged a stretcher bed there on my way from a harvest camp in Worcestershire to one in Cornwall. At 3a.m. I set off to walk to Temple Meads for the 3.45 am to Callington and on my way saw just three people – two Americans and a policeman who asked me

Evelyn Libra in the 1990s.

for my identity card.

Hall photograph was due to be taken after breakfast on 6 June 1944, the day exams commenced, but already rumours had started that this was to be the day of the long awaited 'second front' and those on their way to the first exam in the morning saw the crowds around the Radio Rentals shop in Queen's Road and heard the first news of the D-Day landings in Normandy. Nearly a year later there was even more excitement as we awaited V. E. Day (the end of the war in Europe). At about five o'clock Miss Macleod hoisted the Union flag on the flagpole on the flat roof of Callander. In the course of the evening it was taken as a trophy by the men of Wills. An expedition to reclaim it was led by the Senior Student and, having been unsuccessful, made do with the Manor Hall flag instead. Miss Macleod regarded imperturbably the sight of her students hurtling through the dining room hotly pursued by those from Manor, and having given everyone time to exhaust their high spirits, calmed us down and we proceeded with the programmes long planned for the day. At this distance it seems perhaps a little juvenile, but we were young. We had been through our University careers in the knowledge that we were privileged to be able to continue our studies while so many of our contemporaries were out there fighting, so the release from tension was too great to be resisted.

In the afternoon, those of us who were still in Hall, together with some of the men from Wills, assembled in the JCR to hear Mr Churchill speak on the wireless. We listened attentively and stood for The National Anthem afterwards. That evening we could see bonfires from our windows and could hear the sound of hymns. The next day we attended a University Service of Thanksgiving in the Victoria Rooms, where three weeks later I was to sit my finals.

PAULINE ROBERTS (NÉE CLARK) 1952-1953

My arrival at the beginning of Freshers' Week in September 1952 was hardly auspicious. I had been wandering around Clifton, lugging a heavy suitcase, lost – and nobody I asked could direct me to Clifton Hill House! It was with relief that I eventually approached the imposing front door, but inside I met the rather formidable lady 'Porteress', who informed me that the room I was to share was in the Annexe, Manor House. Happily, established students were there to help bewildered Freshers and I was taken under their wing.

Food was still rationed and, since meals were taken in the main Hall, breakfast-time saw flocks of students making their way through the streets of Clifton, clutching their little dishes of butter and pots of sugar. Those of us who had lab practicals, or 12 o'clock lectures faced a challenging walk up Clifton Hill from the University to 1 o'clock lunch in Hall. It certainly raised the appetite! Friday evening was formal dinner night, when we were expected to wear 'afternoon dresses', and take our turn on the rota for dining at top table. The Warden, Miss Macleod, would process along the dining hall, frequently with her guest Miss Butcher from the History Department. She used to put me in mind of Wallis Simpson, with her slim build and dark bobbed hair.

We would each visit Miss Macleod in her study, briefly, at the beginning of each year (or was it term?). I remember the first time – she said: 'Miss Clark, where is your home?' and when I replied 'Birmingham', she exclaimed that Birmingham was the coldest place she knew and that her home in the far north of Scotland was positively balmy in comparison! Being addressed as 'Miss' by such a senior lady was quite a shock to someone so recently a schoolgirl. After formal dinners, we used to adjourn to the Library (now the Music Room) where coffee was served. It was quite a crush in there, and, having acquired a cup of coffee, it was almost impossible to locate the sugar basin – I eventually gave up trying, and from that day to this have never sweetened my coffee!

There were no evening meals in Hall at the weekend, but instead there was an institution known as 'ration supper'. Each student collected their evening allowance of food earlier in the day – in Manor House it had been brought over on a large tray and left in the Kitchen. It sometimes included a Brains meat pie – could this be the same Brains that now sponsor the Welsh Rugby Team? The Manor House kitchen had no cooking facilities that I remember – we boiled our kettles on a gas ring on the landing (envying those resident in more modern halls, provided with a pull-down gas ring on the top of the gas fires in their own rooms). Heating the meat pie on a plate balanced on the kettle was quite a challenge! (My room mate and I had economised by not buying a saucepan.)

Manor House kitchen was a warm and cosy place, but sparsely furnished – an old detached leather bucket seat from a car was the most comfortable place to sit. Our House Meetings took place there, and it was my favourite place for burning the midnight oil on the eve of exams. The front door was firmly shut and locked at 11 pm but some obliging students with ground-floor rooms had been known to open their windows to let in late returners! The Clifton Hill House formal dance took place in the Autumn Term. Having to invite a partner was all the more awkward before I had got to know many people. Nevertheless it was enjoyable, with overtones of a Jane Austen occasion. Contrasting with this was the experience of the annual Rag Procession. I remember one year the Clifton Hill House theme was 'Gypsies', and I particularly enjoyed wearing male dress complete with flat cap, neckerchief and tobacco pipe! Another year our float was filled with 'The Clifton Sweeties' – I went as 'Butterscotch' with tartan skirt and yellow top, but the costume I admired most was worn by someone in brown trousers and top, with a red satin cummerbund – a 'chocolate cigar'!

One vivid memory from 1953 was of how I 'celebrated' the Coronation. Clifton Hill House was half empty, as some people had been invited out to watch on TV and many had finished their exams and gone home. Mine were not finished, and the Warden gave me special permission to invite my boy friend to my room for a picnic lunch and an all-day session listening to the Coronation radio broadcast! As the first member of my family to go to University, and in a city I didn't know, I found the Clifton Hill House could be a refuge and retreat. Yet friendship and social activity there broadened my experience and has left me with many happy memories.

ANNE GRAY 1953-1956

We mustn't say these are our happiest days,
Just our happiest days so far.

When I think of Bristol I always hear the lyrics from *Salad Days*, the Bristol Old Vic musical which later had a long run in the West End. CHH played a large part in making my undergraduate days happy. Apart from living in a gracious Georgian house, albeit dilapidated as was everything in the UK at that time, I made lasting friendships. In October 1953 I found a blitz-scarred city. Bomb sites, some cleared, some with rubble, lined Park Street. The University's Great Hall, site of our matriculation ceremony, had suffered considerable damage and still awaited repair when we graduated in 1956. Elsewhere the desecration of Old Bristol by planners and architects was well under way, completing the work the Luftwaffe had begun. The country was still in the grip of austerity, but it was beginning to loosen. We registered our ration books with the Ministry of Food as CHH residents. From the bursar we received butter rations which we carried to meals. Rationing ended by 1956 but CHH food, British institutional cooking at its worst, did not improve. Climbing Clifton Hill after noon lectures we were greeted with lumpy mashed potatoes, overcooked leeks or beetroot covered in floury white sauce, and meat, if any, sliced so fine it was nearly transparent. Vegetarian supper (cabbage, grated cheese, raisins) invariably drove us down the hill to the Nightingale café for egg and chips (one shilling and sixpence). But we were young, hungry and short of cash; we usually ate whatever appeared on the table.

First-year students were kept busy. Evening meals were not served in the dining-room at weekends. Instead there was

Clifton Hill House Dance, November 1956. Anne Gray is in the middle.

And I remember fondly the warden, Miss Macleod, whose soft Scottish accent immediately endeared her to me. In our first year we saw her after breakfast to ask permission to go out after dinner; the expression on her face, no words necessary, let us know if our social life might be detrimental to our academic ambitions. For formal dinner on Fridays, she wore, every week for three years, a floor-length skirt in heavy satin with a fishtail and a multi-coloured blouse. With her 1930s bobbed hair, she resembled Gertrude Lawrence in *Private Lives,* a comparison she probably would not have enjoyed. With a few exceptions, she had a talent for choosing compatible room mates and she was a great resource in time of trouble. I envied friends who studied psychology with her. Clifton Hill House, I loved it.

Don't turn round, we're outward bound,
And we said we wouldn't look back.

Yet I do!

Anne graduated in 1956 (B.A. in History) She now lives in California.

ANNE MARTIN-CARPENTER 1953-1957

I arrived at Bristol University in October 1953 to read History, the first of my family to attend University. I had little idea of what to expect. Luckily, two school friends also chose to attend Bristol, though neither was in hall and both were reading other subjects. I was in Manor House, in those days an annexe of Clifton Hill House. I shared a room with another Londoner, also reading History.

An early memory is presenting my ration book to a local government official so I could be registered for rations. I

'ration supper'. We distributed the rations (e.g. an egg, a crumpet and an apple). Food parcels from home saved the day. On Sundays we washed up after lunch. The kitchens were a revelation, the unpleasant side of eighteenth-century living: huge, metal-lined sinks full of scummy water in which to scrub pots, with primitive versions of dishwashers for the plates.

So many memories! Our spacious rooms contained old but good furniture, lovingly polished by Rose, a character with a strong Bristol accent; there were gas fires (use limited to three hours a day). Sunday breakfast was the best meal of the week, with excellent coffee. Maud, another character, presided over the dining-room. I remember the annual ball in the autumn, the Hall plays, Hall floats in Rag week, the summer coffee dances, the endless cups of instant coffee with friends setting the world to rights. Most of all, I think of the friends.

Clifton Hill House dray in Rag Week, 1956.

queued with other Freshers in a large hall in the Centre. (At breakfast time we carried our butter ration from Manor House to Clifton Hill House.) By Christmas 1953 rationing ended.

In hall, the first-year students had duties; all arranged by rota. On Sundays the kitchen staff cooked the lunch, then left. We first years washed up. Clifton Hill House is an elegant eighteenth-century building, its kitchens in 1953 were below stairs. The sinks were huge, deep and lead lined. Washing up liquid was in the future. Little pieces of soap in mesh, metal containers with handles could be shaken to offset the grease in the water. The best tip was given to us by the elderly mother of one of the kitchen staff. Fill a large metal water jug with hot soapy water and soak the cutlery in it. Otherwise one's arm went down into the water, up to the elbow, to fish out the knives, forks and spoons lurking in the depths. There was a primitive form of dishwasher/conveyor belt to help with some of the plates.

Another duty was distributing 'ration supper'. On Saturday and Sunday no evening meal was provided. Instead items of food were collected and delivered by first years to every room. Recipients were supposed to leave a plate on which said items could be put. (The story of one student returning to find a slice of veal and ham pie on her eiderdown, no plate being found, is probably apocryphal.) The food was fairly basic, eggs to be boiled or scrambled, pie, salad. Food parcels from home were appreciated, supplementing what we could afford to buy out of our grants.

On Fridays dinner was formal. All students attended and took it in turns to sit at High Table, having escorted the Warden and sub-Wardens into the Dining Hall. The others rose as they entered, and stayed standing until all those at High Table were seated.

Meals in hall were not exciting. We in Britain were still living in 'austerity' after all. I remember a dish of boiled, sliced beetroot in a white sauce. The sauce turned pink as the serving spoon grappled with the beetroot. Another treat was lentil cake. It was dry and lacking in flavour. It was served with salad.

If my friends and I had 1/6d (7.5p) to spare, we would go to a small café called The Nightingale, near Berkeley Square, for egg, chips and a cup of instant coffee – bliss!

My memories of Bristol are very happy ones. To a Londoner the snow on Clifton Downs was amazing, so deep, so pure, so unlike the grey slush I was used to. The Downs in winter snow were magical.

I remember cheering Winston Churchill, our Chancellor, on a wet winter's day in Colston Hall, with my freezing feet tucked into my fur gloves.

Above all, I remember the friends I made, some of whom are still close to me, nearly sixty years on. The University of Bristol – what a great start to my adult life.

Dressed up for Rag Day, 1954.

PEGGY STEMBRIDGE LATE 1950S – LIFE IN CLIFTON WOOD ANNEXE

Clifton Wood House, down the hill from CHH, was built in the 1720s, probably by the carpenter architect George Tully. In the late 1950s it became one of the two annexes for students from CHH, but apart from its impressive entrance hall and handsome staircase with the rare folding hound gate, it had lost the elegance it had when rented for a few seasons at the Hotwells by the Countess of Huntingdon, or when inhabited by the rich banker Levi Ames and his family or even when Queen Mary took tea with the Dean of Bristol during World War II. By the 1960s when it housed a tutor and 22 students, it lacked modern facilities, and was in a dismal state of decoration and repair. The large rooms were shared by two students, unlike Goldney annexe where the main rooms had been divided into cubicles rather like horse-boxes. There was no communal kitchen or laundry, but personal laundry could be taken to the washing machines in CHH. The few bathrooms were Victorian and draughty. Breakfast and supper were provided in CHH dining room, except for Sunday supper, when simple rations were handed out at lunchtime to be taken back down the hill.

Responsibilities for students do not change much over the years: consulting about work, personal problems, exam stress or illness, but Clifton Wood probably had more domestic emergencies – power failures, water leaks, intruders attempting to climb in windows, obscene telephone calls on the one phone in the cupboard (no mobiles then). For services on 24-hour call for our own students, and on duty for the whole of CHH and locking up two evenings a week (a chore on winter nights), perhaps two weekends a term, and a morning a week issuing keys or passes, we tutors were allowed half our residence fees in university term time. For a tutor not accustomed to communal living, it was a demanding, interesting and unforgotten 'spare-time' experience.

I hope some students remember with pleasure social occasions in the smaller community in CWH: pancake parties, with the cooking done in relays by two or three squeezed in to the tutor's tiny antiquated kitchen, parties with quantities of Cheddar strawberries or picnic lunches in the overgrown garden, sunbathing well out of sight on the roof. Home-made cakes for tea always seemed to be popular, the small payments for which eventually paid for the repair of the round window in Goldney grotto. A more homely atmosphere was also provided by the small cat that adopted us, and slept on essays or in front of gas fires, but also stole ham from a Christmas party, in spite of being well fed on scraps from the CHH kitchen.

All this was a long time ago, and where now are the dozens of successful lawyers, medics, linguists and others who count a year in a dilapidated eighteenth-century house as part of their university experience?

SYLVIA BARRY EARLY 1960s

Looking back and, almost certainly at the time too, we all felt very privileged to be in Clifton Hill House. We were near the university, near Clifton village and within walking distance of Ashton Court and Leigh Woods. We all made many lasting friendships. The rooms in the then new wing were pretty small but well furnished and had superb views across the city. We spent a lot of time in each other's rooms, drinking tea and, on Sundays, listening to 'Top Of The Pops'. Some of us had radios but nothing more sophisticated! Very few of us came by car and so we all had trunks that came by train and had to be stored.

The warden, Miss Macleod, was a very thin, gaunt, nervy strict and academic lady with glasses and tweeds. Rumour has it that she had a live grenade on her windowsill! She felt very much that she was 'in loco parentis'. Men were NOT allowed in the rooms and a friend remembers what difficulty she had convincing the authorities that the young man in question was her brother! I have a vague feeling that men were allowed in on special occasions but my husband, who was then my boy friend, maintains he never saw the inside of my room! Equally strict were closing times and we had to get a special pass to be out late.

Many of our memories revolved around food! We had breakfast and an evening meal, which on Friday was formal. We had our turn to sit at the High Table. At the weekend we had 'raw rations' for some of the meals: eggs and bacon, which we could cook in one of the kitchens on each floor. Sunday lunch was a roast. People who were in the annexe remember toasting crumpets on a gas fire.

Our memories of laundry are vague but we were only allowed to send one sheet a week and if you missed the time it wasn't accepted.

We were mostly very unsophisticated and didn't seem to mind the boarding school atmosphere. Our friends in digs were very envious and had some horror stories of their landladies. The most important aspect of our time there was the friendships we forged, friendships that are still going strong.

ANN STARK (NÉE BUSSEY) 1962-1964

The end of my first year in Bristol found my room-mate Gill Garner and myself searching for somewhere to live. Our annexe, Manor House, we had learned rather late in the day, was due to be handed over to Manor Hall. We had suggested to Miss Macleod that we might be transferred with it (ever hopeful, but to be disappointed). She did not take kindly to this idea and so we found ourselves visiting one set of dismal bedsitters after another. Surprisingly just before the new term began Miss Macleod offered us a double room in Clifton Wood House which we gratefully accepted and with alacrity!

Thus were to begin what probably were the two happiest years of my life. There was, of course, the culmination of this happy idyll to worry about – finals! I was never a 'day' person and I remember the long hours at night when the rest of CWH was asleep and I was at work on history essays. The basic research for these was done in the Arts Library where books were loaned for either a morning, afternoon or evening session, such was their popularity (and scarcity) when a particular essay was set. Woe betide the person who returned a book late. All around you in the dark recesses of the downstairs library would be History students frantically speed-reading a book of perhaps 700 pages, searching for and then scribbling notes down of what they hoped were relevant excerpts. These would form the basis of the essay to be written up later. I remember that on essay writing night my bedroom floor would be covered with slips of paper as they were copied or rejected. There would be perhaps four or five 'fair' copies made of an essay before the final one. How I envy modern students with their word-processing computers and the ability to cut and paste. Perhaps, though, modernity brings other problems with model essays on every topic for sale and worries about cheating.

It is said that everybody of a certain age remembers where they were when they learned that President Kennedy had been assassinated and I am no exception. I was in my room writing a history essay (as usual burning the much later than midnight oil) and also with one ear listening to an 'American Forces in Europe' late night pop song show on my transistor radio. Suddenly the show stopped and the awful news was broadcast. I was flabbergasted and incredibly saddened but could not share this with anyone else – they, unlike me, were all fast asleep!

As finals loomed ever closer then my files of lecture notes were refined and superfined to such a degree that every topic was reduced to key words or phrases on white postcards. These travelled with me everywhere! I recall last minute revision rushing down the steps to Constitution Hill, the last desperate trip to the cloakroom under the great stone stairs in the Wills Building and fervent prayers – and yes, I did get that degree. However, although it is now almost fifty years ago, I still dream of taking my finals. In these nightmares I am standing outside the exam room and no one will tell me what the exam is about and of course I have done no revision. I guess that many others still get such anxiety dreams.

After our first year in Manor House our new accommodation was a great improvement. CWH was bright and cheerful after the decaying Manor House although we now realised why no money had been spent on repairs or modernisation of the latter. Our new room was on the first floor and from its elegant Queen Anne bay window we enjoyed unsurpassed views of the front door and a preview of visitors (ours and other people's!). Immediately opposite was a cloakroom with W.C. and a large washbasin which, because we were in the nearest room, became rather like our own 'en-suite'! Even better was the extra room we 'acquired' halfway up the narrow wooden back stairs and equipped with two easy chairs. It was said to be unsafe for permanent occupation because of the danger of fire but it was just the job for Gill and myself in our role of Hall decorators/rag preparation prop providers etc. In this room we cut out silver paper silhouettes of Cinderella-type coaches, crinoline ladies and young gallants to decorate CHH's dining and common rooms for the Mozart-themed Hall Ball of 1962. A year later saw us constructing Taj Mahal silhouettes and sinewy ladies draped in real saris for an Indian theme. We provided the props for a circus float in spring 1963 for the Rag procession and in 1964 gigantic papier mâché heads which we wore to represent lawyers in the *Fanny Hill* case which was a current issue.

CWH was a wonderful place to explore. No door was locked (student vandalism and theft was unheard of then) and this allowed Gill and myself to thoroughly explore attics, including the out-of-door flat roof spaces, and of course the cellars. It did not take us long to realise that the wine cellar, accessed from the front hall, went under only half of the house and we were determined to find the rest. Gill eventually did this by going out through a downstairs cloakroom window and dropping four feet or so down into a small courtyard in which she could see the cellar entrance. Unfortunately, during her exploration, a gentleman friend of the then sub-warden decided to use the

cloakroom for rather a long time after having first closed the window. There was no way I could prevent him and Gill had no way of knowing that it was not I playing a trick on her. Fortunately she chose not to reveal her presence and as she was armed with a box of matches she decided to continue her exploration. Later, having regained *terra firma*, so to speak, she revealed that she had seen several iron fireplaces and mantelpieces, presumably removed from the student rooms above and at that time virtually worthless. Many years later in the 1990s another search by Mrs Burnside showed that these now valuable items had gone! What a shame, but perhaps somewhere today in Bristol, or elsewhere, someone sits in front of a CWH fireplace and values its appearance.

Another place that we got to know intimately was Goldney Grotto. Surprisingly we had not visited Goldney in our first year but now the gardens were more accessible as they were adjacent to CWH. We first approached the grotto from its rear service tunnel unaware that this was its purpose. We were totally amazed when we emerged in the grotto itself, complete with its shell-encrusted walls and statues. We were soon to become familiar with the narrow passages which ran behind the waterfall. In later years these were locked to prevent damage and the grotto itself was only opened on special occasions so we were the lucky ones. The gardens themselves were delightful with the orangery, gazebos and lily ponds. We had picnics and lunch parties with our friends and played croquet, in what now looking back seems like a golden age.

For two consecutive years Gill and I were responsible for organising the Goldney Ball – a magic affair with dancing on a raised floor on the lawns, refreshments in the orangery and tea lights in jam jars along the border walks. The dance floor was (unknown to most of the dancers) supported on metal waste bins borrowed from Wills Hall. Apparently the gentlemen there needed stout bins, unlike we frailer creatures in CHH!

During the week all our meals were taken in CHH which meant a short walk up the hill. I cannot say that I attended all the weekday breakfasts and certainly not at weekends, but I was present for lunch and dinner. The quality of the meals was always excellent and fortunately by my second year there was more food available. This had not been the case during our first year when Gill and I had supplemented our meagre fare by growing mustard and cress on every available surface! As we were part of the new intake in the vast 1961 expansion of CHH perhaps the kitchens hadn't got used to catering for such numbers to begin with. Weekends, however, were a different matter and we were required to cook our own Saturday and Sunday evening meals with rations provided. The latter were delivered to a ground floor pantry in CWH and early collection was advisable. Every week someone would be unlucky and there would be recriminations over the missing food.

Cooking presented problems as there were only three gas rings, one on each floor. In the early 1960s we had no toasters, electric kettles, microwaves or refrigerators and I wonder now how we managed. Gill created a food warmer with an Oxo tin and a nightlight and this allowed us to have a meal that was uniformly hot though it had been cooked in stages and on different floors! Needless to say I don't remember any overweight students in CWH.

As I have been writing this article memories have been flooding in and far too many for me to write down. It was a wonderful time and over too quickly. Gill and I have remained firm friends – how wise of Miss Macleod to put us together almost 50 years ago. We were each other's bridesmaids and our sons now in their thirties are also friends. My elder daughter passed through CHH as an undergraduate and then returned for a time as a tutor with Mrs Burnside. I have returned on several occasions to revisit CWH but now, sadly, it has been sold and is no longer part of the University.

HARRIETT BRADLEY, 1963
MEMORIES OF CLIFTON HILL HOUSE IN THE 'SWINGING 60S'
I arrived at Clifton Hill House in October 1963, accompanied by mother, father and a massive trunk. Things did not get off to a propitious start. I had been assigned a room at the end of A floor, the top level of the recently opened new building. Once the parents left, I started to unpack the trunk and rearrange my possessions in the newly painted and furbished room. I placed my books on the bookshelf fixed to the wall above the bed, then started to hang my clothes in the fitted wardrobe. Suddenly there was a terrible bang. The shelf had come off the wall and the end had crashed on to one of my most prized possessions, a huge Grundig reel-to-reel tape-recorder inherited from my uncle. I had precious tapes of popular music recorded from Radio Luxembourg. The shelf had crashed right through the lid of the box and bored a hole right down into the works.

Immediately I was labelled a troublemaker by the Domestic Bursar. Why had I put heavy items, such as books, on the shelf? I pointed out that as a student of English Literature it was rather likely that I should perceive a shelf as designed to hold these essential study aids! I responded that the shelf had obviously been insecurely fixed and that the Hall should pay me for the repair to the recorder. It took a phone call from my father, who pointed out that if I myself, rather than the recorder, had been lying on the bed my skull would have been crushed like an eggshell. Subsequently all the shelves in the block were moved on to a different wall of the room… However, the Bursar never really forgave me, and when later that year I contracted an ulcerated throat which was agonisingly painful, she refused to call the doctor, suggesting that I was suffering from a hangover and trying to get out of lectures…

As for the recorder, the Hall insurance paid for a repair but it never worked properly again.

Meanwhile, social life at CHH was coming along nicely. Whether by accident or design, a whole batch of first-year English students had been given rooms on A floor. Besides myself there were Kate, Catherine, Jan, Brigid and Rae. Quickly we became the A-floor gang. Other English students were over in the lovely Goldney Hall, at that time a small annexe to CHH; while we had single rooms, they were sharing – Mariette, Val and Wendy became good friends, but were all a little more sophisticated and confident than the A-floor gang – we were grammar-school girls from rather sheltered backgrounds, and none of us had ever had a boyfriend.

In that respect we fitted well into the virginal world of CHH. We were allowed to have male visitors only on Wednesdays and Saturdays, entertaining them to tea in the common room, with its armchairs and televisions; they were never allowed to visit our rooms. So if we wanted to learn about the intricacies of romance we had to visit the male halls, where no such restrictions pertained.

This regime was presided over by the redoubtable figure of the Warden, Miss Macleod. Miss Macleod wore tweed suits, with thick stockings and sensible shoes. She was thin and neatly built, with black haircut severely and spoke with a clipped Scots accent. We were all terrified of her: the main contact was collecting pass-out keys if we wanted to stay out beyond lockup time in the evening. There was a strong sense that if we asked for these privileges too often we would be viewed with disapproval, for such late excursions were seen as incompatible with a serious life of study. Although going to ask for a pass-key was an intimidating experience, with hindsight I suspect it was a shrewd way for the Warden to get to know her students individually while keeping a bit of an eye on them.

Despite these constraints, we enjoyed our life at CHH so much that the A-floor gang opted to stay in hall for a second year rather than venture out into the wider world of student flats. While I can recall the painful nature of Saturday nights, when girls in curlers and dressing gowns prepared for their dates and the rest of us sat around miserably hoping that the next time the telephone rang it would be some admirer asking us out, most of the time we were engaged in a thrilling and vigorous world of female friendships. Over endless cups of coffee we discussed our lecturers, our fellow students, our essays, favourite books, the films, we had seen the outings we had been on. Kate read *Winnie-the-Pooh* aloud to us, with an array of voices; we jumped up and down to the Beatles and to Carmina Burana and we fell about the room in bouts of hysterical laughter. I discovered Bob Dylan and introduced him to the others. The talented Kate organised us into a cabaret performed in the common room: we performed our version of the Beatles 'She loves you Yeah, yeah, yeah, YEAH' and sang Kate's own version of 'A lover and his lass':

> It was a beatnik and his bike
> And they were on a burn-up, like
> A doing the ton
> All down the MI
> It was such fab-u-lous fun!

The lack of men did not inhibit our capacity for fun, although at a lively party held by Mariette and Val in Goldney a couple were smuggled in. This was the first occasion on which I experienced being (literally) legless with drink, after mixing a toxic brew of British sherry, wine, cider and whisky and defiantly drinking it. My more sensible friends had virtually to carry me across the road back to Hall and up to A floor. Luckily, my mind has blanked out the memory of the following morning.

Twice a week we had formal dinners. Miss Macleod and her staff sat in state at the High Table; we all had to wear gowns and stand while the Warden read grace before the meal: 'for what we are about to receive may The Lord make us truly thankful.' As far as I can remember we were thankful for the food (as now) was pretty good; beef olives were a favourite. But, in true student fashion, we sometimes cut hall meals in order to savour the delights of the student union cafeteria – egg, beans and chips!

We all worked quite hard at our studies, and to some

extent the female enclave of CHH offered a welcome relief from the other world of romance and heartache with which we were slowly engaging. We acted in plays, sang in OpSoc and the university choir. The A-floor gang played the troubled teenagers in *The Crucible*, a Hall play organised jointly with the young men from Burwalls (then another hall of residence) which was produced by Catherine. I recall putting the metal waste bin from my room on my head when dressing up as a soldier for the Clifton Hill House Rag Day float. We met young men, went on dates, fell in love, started 'going steady'. But while the men came and went, the female friendships remained steady. In some senses, I think the stern Miss Macleod was probably pleased with her girls. I remember encountering her late one night in the hall library where I was labouring on an essay. There was an approving nod. It was all very different from student life nowadays! But, no doubt about it, those years were charmed – we had the time of our young lives. The third year of our stay – cut loose from the apron strings of hall routine – would be something else again, with very different challenges.

Harriet Bradley is now Professor of Sociology, Bristol.

Senior Student's Report 1965-1966

This has been a memorable year and a sad one. After being Warden of Clifton Hill house for thirty years, Miss J. W. Macleod retired to her home in Scotland at the end of the autumn term. The news of her departure came as a complete surprise to all her students, both past and present. She has done so much for us in all her time here that it seems impossible to envisage Clifton without her. She has been a friend and adviser to everyone. To those who had the privilege of working with her as members of Hall Committee, her retirement is a great loss. Her fund of knowledge and wisdom on all matters in and out of Hall rendered most committees superfluous. The extent to which we all relied on her is realised only now that she has left. I hope most sincerely that her retirement is a happy one and that she will visit us when she can.

Although the events of the remainder of the year are rather overshadowed by Miss Macleod's departure, I will give a brief summary. In the summer term of 1965 a lull in activities ensued, as usual, for finals. Their completion was celebrated by a successful Ball held in Goldney Gardens. In the autumn term we were installed as the new committee to welcome the first-year students. The Freshers' Entertainment, on a theme of 'education', was most amusing. As Miss Macleod remarked, it is amazing that in thirty years no theme has ever been repeated. The committee gave a social evening for the other halls committees. This took the place of the former annual reciprocal dinners which were abolished when the number of halls increased to seven. Towards the end of term we held a very successful ball, decorated on a Christmas theme. The term culminated in the annual Christmas Dinner and Carol Concert, when we presented Miss Macleod with an engraved silver cigarette box.

This spring term is proceeding smoothly, although we have no Warden. Miss Carpenter is very ably standing in until next term when Mrs Baldock arrives to take up her post as Warden. At the time of writing, the Hall elections and Rag Week are due soon. In all, I think we can say that 1965/66 will be a memorable year in CHH's history.

Senior Student's Report 1966-1967

In October three new rooms, two doubles and a single came into use as the basement in Old Clifton was converted and decorated into 'garden rooms'.

The Ball was the big event of this term and took place a fortnight before Christmas. The decorations were planned to give an atmosphere of winter but it was contradicted by the warmth and enjoyment of 250 guests. It was voted a great success despite the tardy arrival of a depleted dance band whose saxophonist had 'flu and the drummer got lost en route. A special delight was the singing of the 'Twelve Days of Christmas' by six girls, who wrote words appropriate to Hall life – for example 'five men visitors... and a duplicate key.'

There was no Hall play last year owing to lack of interest in Hall, but the Clifton Hill pedal car did very well in its class in the 24-hour race during Rag and the float was gay and colourful. It was a representation of 'Odyseus and the Sirens', but almost came to grief only one hundred yards from Hall when the 'mast' of the boat got caught up in telephone wires across the road. As the entire telecommunications system of the city seemed in danger it was thought advisable to lower the mast in the public interest. Hall did particularly well during the year in the Debating Society's competition and we hope for further success this year.

President's Report 1967-1968

I am pleased to report that life in Clifton Hill has been great this year. For the first time the new committee, rather than beginning its new term of office in the autumn, took over at the start of the summer. This meant that not only could the old Committee feel free to get down to finals but also that the new Committee had a chance to form their policy and get to know each other before the influx of the new students. This year also we decided to change the title of Senior Student to that of President as this seemed more in line with a democratic system. It would also, we thought, obviate the confusion which faced me three years ago when I had visions of being introduced to the oldest person in the building. Surrounded by decaying eighteenth-century stonework and having a too fertile imagination, I was somewhat intimidated by the idea!

In October the Committee worked very hard to welcome an intake of about 100 first years – showing them around the University departments and places of interest in Bristol, and offering advice on the necessity to work, accompanied by the inevitable mugs of coffee. A little later in the term the first years planned their own cider party in the JCR and entertained members of Wills and Burwalls – an event which was highly successful, not simply because of the opportunity it offered for meeting male students, but also because its organisation united all the Freshers and demanded the participation of the shyest.

With Christmas came another lovely Ball – one of the highlights of our year. Once again the JCR was transformed miraculously into a ballroom – appreciated by the romantics among us, while a delicious candle-lit feast more than satisfied our ever-hungry partners. This year too, our Carol Concert, after a superb Christmas Dinner, was greatly enhanced by a mixed choir, and several members of Burwalls enticed by the promise of mincepies and coffee, encouraged us to continue singing long after the SCR had left us. By 11p.m. we were all hoarse! Unfortunately the Carol Concert was the last occasion on which Dr Pye will be visiting us en masse in her official role as Chairman of the House Committee but we shall look forward to seeing her in Clifton Hill in the future despite her retirement from the post.

This Christmas too, we had the good idea of decorating the tree, not with the usual baubles, but with presents for children – bought and wrapped by each member of Hall.

The result was particularly rewarding – the tree looked lovely and later we were able to send two huge boxes of gifts to Dr Barnardo's.

But life has not been all parties! We are pleased to report that several girls have taken leading roles in Drama Department and Operatic productions and at the moment a small cast is being selected for a Hall play, written and produced by a second-year student in Hall. Our swimming team is extremely energetic this year, and we even have a staunch rugger team who, apart from inflicting grievous injuries upon brave teams from Stoke Bishop, seem to win (by almost fair means) with astonishing regularity!

As well as having a particularly united JCR Committee, this year has seen the innovation of Presidents' Meetings – informal gatherings of the Presidents of the eight Halls of Residence in order to discuss matters of general Hall policy. We have succeeded in getting truer representation in Union affairs, a small column in *Nonesuch* and, primarily, a much better idea of how other halls work. This unity between halls is essential and we hope future Presidents will continue to hold these meetings.

Last, but not least, we have joined Mrs Baldock and the SCR in giving a number of dinner parties in Clifton Hill for 'interesting guests'. These, though we say it ourselves, have been great fun. Last term we entertained, amongst others, the Vice-Chancellor and his wife, and this week Professor and Mrs Hewer came and entertained us with a delightful story about a dolphin. Those of us who had not heard the dolphin saga before listened in wide-eyed amazement...and we are still pondering the mysterious question – 'What *was* Dr Wiltshire doing in the potting shed?'

ROBERTA MACDONALD, PRESIDENT'S REPORT 1968-1969

I am writing as a second-year student about to hand the presidency to a first-year girl who will take up office next term. This, I think, will be the pattern in future, for girls in their final year are increasingly reluctant to shoulder this responsibility which can well be undertaken in the second year.

Second announcement: visiting hours now stand at 11am to 10.30pm every day. I say this not because it has been a world shattering event but because looking through past notes it seems to have been the cause championed each year – and I thought you might like to know.

This gradual relaxation of restrictions is a reflection of the climate of opinion in the University generally and makes for a more pleasing atmosphere in a Hall of Residence. I like to think that a lack of unrest is indicative of contentment not indifference.

Indeed, the support for Hall activities does show that apathy is not as rampant as is sometimes imagined. Volunteers were not slow in coming forward to build the caterpillar and tread the weary path of the Rag procession. Twelve stalwarts manfully endured the 24-hour pedal car race and though this year we couldn't raise a rugger team, our debating skills were revived after lying untapped for some while. Our Christmas Ball, too, was a great success (naturally!) and I am sure our kitchen staff must be the best of the Bristol halls – witness one Christmas dinner which was something of a marvel and formed part of a lovely evening of carol singing by candlelight.

But perhaps one of the most memorable events of the past year has been the Soirée – a formal musical evening where we tried to recapture something of the atmosphere of the eighteenth century in the authentic setting of Clifton Hill's library and old common room. The room was softened by the light of candles. A cider-cup was served throughout the evening (we couldn't afford punch!) while we listened to madrigals, to instrumental pieces, to poetry and prose reading – do you know what love-secrets the *Spectator* revealed in the eighteenth century? We strolled in the garden in the mid-evening, each of us in our long dresses and our partners in dinner jackets, and as we finished our bath buns and hot chocolate we listened to a rousing chorus of 'Rule Britannia'!

It was a very beautiful evening and we hope again to capture that unusually dignified atmosphere in Goldney House next term – a fitting farewell for this is the last year in which we shall enjoy the house and gardens which will form part of the new Goldney Hall. No – they're not touching the garden nor pulling the house down – not the outside anyway! And to our loss Mrs Baldock will be ensconced in the wood-panelled room downstairs...

Helen Conway 1979-1982

I feel enormously privileged to have lived at Clifton Hill House whilst I was at Bristol University, although I do appreciate that all students have an affiliation to 'their' Hall and believe 'theirs' is best. Here are a few of my recollections of my time there and the influence that living in Hall had on my life.

When I was offered a place to study Mechanical Engineering at Bristol my immediate priority was to look to which Hall of Residence I should apply. To me Clifton Hill House stood out as the Jewel in the Crown! It accommodated boys as well as girls (important to someone from an all-girls' school!), was within ten minutes walk of the University, close to the spectacular Bridge designed by my favourite engineer, not to mention the surrounding village of Clifton which is wonderful, and was a place full of char-acter with a sympathetic blend of modern accommodation within the environs of a beautiful historic house dating from 1747.

I vividly remember arriving at Clifton Hill House on my first day at University and my initial impression was 'Wow'. The entrance into reception was very welcoming and impressive. Understandably the scene was somewhat chaotic with parents delivering their offspring who were both apprehensive and excited about the new chapter they were opening in their lives. Amongst the parents bidding farewell and the mêlée of trunks there were introductions that, in some cases, were the beginning of lifetime friend-ships. I am very fortunate to continue to enjoy the friendship of both of my neighbours whom I met on that first day.

For many, but not all, Clifton Hill House was their first experience of living away from home. The comfortable ambiance, especially evident in the original buildings, created an atmosphere of security but with independence right from the start that lasted throughout one's life at Bristol University. I do not remember an overload of rules and regulations, more a feeling of being able to take responsibility for oneself. Miss Sheila Brennan was the Warden during my time there and when I became Hall President towards the end of my first year I had regular contact with her. She was a kind person who knew all of us and had the ability to make sure that standards and decorum were maintained whilst showing understanding and reassurance where necessary. This was especially evident in our early days there whilst we made the transi-tion from school to student life.

I certainly felt that I was part of a community at Clifton Hill House and the experience of living, eating and social-ising (there must have been some studying somewhere!)

with such an eclectic mix of students opened one's mind and broadened one's outlook at this stage in our young adult lives. We respected and appreciated the views and talents of our fellow students and this was influential in forming our future aspirations and relationships in all aspects of our lives.

Inevitably, in a community like this, the social side played an important part. I had not long been living there before my friends and I had discovered the delights of the local hostelry, the Coronation Tap. In Clifton Hill House there was a bar run by the JCR where you could socialise after a day's lectures/studying. We took responsibility for this seriously and were therefore given a level of autonomy that made us feel it was ours. Each Hall held formal dinners and a Ball, organised by the JCR in consultation with the Warden and Bursar, and these were well supported by residents. There was some rivalry between the Halls as to whose Ball was best and, naturally, ours was. In my first year we were fortunate enough to have a group of musicians in Hall who 'got together' and in the modern terminology would be described as a Genesis tribute band. They played at our Hall Ball and other events and always drew a large crowd. They were extremely good and I have always been grateful that they introduced me to the music of Genesis (since then I have always been a passionate fan). I think they called themselves Double Two and sadly split up when one of their number who was studying languages went off to study abroad for a year.

Perhaps the most spectacular social event in our Hall was the Summer Garden Party. It had an air of sophistication to be drinking Pimms in the beautiful gardens with the Georgian façade in the background. It was a truly magnificent setting and we seemed to be lucky with the weather. I believe that life at Clifton Hill House had a very positive influence on the early part of my adult life. I benefitted from the experience of being part of a community and able to take responsibility with the security, support and friendship of the people around me combined with living in such wonderful surroundings. I am looking forward to returning for the Centenary weekend particularly as my friends and I have booked to stay in the same rooms that we enjoyed there as students. We might look a little older but we are going to relive many happy memories and hopefully renew some acquaintances.

TIM LEVELL 1988-1990

I remember on my first day being slightly overawed by all those who had clearly spent several years at boarding school and were very adept at shifting their life to life in an educational institution for months at a time. I packed far too much, but also loved 'customising' my room, so had lots of posters and loads of clothes and lots of books and loads of tapes and CDs and so on. Many more CHH residents just had one of those classic boarding school-style trunks, which their parents lugged into their bedroom, they were unpacked in a day and their bedroom wasn't hugely personalised.

They were also in and out of each other's rooms immediately, swapping stories and finding out more about each other (I was in Fry Wing). I was a bit more into 'my space' and wanted to 'nest' in my own room.

That said, I also remember that the standard joke was that all you needed to survive the first week and make friends was instant coffee and chocolate HobNobs. They were the biscuit of choice for all Freshers, and the perfect way to get to know each other.

Weekdays were of course packed full with social events – I think Tuesday and Thursday were the key social nights.

Friday and Saturday, by contrast, were surprisingly slow, because a lot of people went away for the weekend. I remember the reasonably equipped Fry Wing kitchens were always pretty empty at weekends, with just me cooking pasta or chilli. Most other people seemed to be out on the town – or to have gone home.

One of my vivid memories, which I'm sure doesn't happen any more, was queuing for the phone to ring home and talk about how things were. I probably rang once a week and talked for about half an hour – even if people were tut-tutting outside the phone booth. With mobiles, I imagine those phone booths rarely exist or are so sought-after.

Another that struck me was that this was the time when Annie Burnside first took over the hall, and every term we would come back, intrigued to know which bit of the hall had been restored to a bit more Georgian glamour. First it was the entrance hall – with hotly-debated Amtico-style flooring – then it was the rooms with the piano and the Print Gallery. It seemed as if the University was able to spend money to restore CHH, and of course we were all very proud of our hall and its grand Palladian splendour. We were all delighted that CHH was being restored to its former glory. I think many students were so used to an institution mentality that the idea that a Warden would care enough about the fabric to improve it as Annie did was just wholly unexpected – but also something which people very much liked!

It was just a bit of a pity that we didn't live in the nice bit! Fry Wing wasn't at all historic, so the restoration never seemed to get that far – the main house was the main beneficiary at my time. I'm sure it's all been glammed up a lot since then.

The JCR was a popular place to hang out, even if the bar's takings often seemed to be siphoned off by whoever was working behind the bar (and there were lots of willing volunteers!). The JCR elections were hotly contested, as I know only too well, as I stood for election in my second term. I got elected, after a massive poster campaign, which included teaser posters as well as straightforward ridiculing of my opponent. We managed to create some great events, with a ball and summer party – the summer drinks on the main hall terrace always made us poverty-stricken students dressed in our charity-shop chic feel like we owned this multi-million pound estate. But perhaps my most lasting legacy was to introduce the first vending machine – a Coke machine. I was passionate about this Coke machine and was delighted with how much money it made for the JCR. It seemed so glamorous, back in the 1980s, to be able to buy a Coca-Cola at any time of day or night. Now I expect it just seems a bit tawdry.

One of the funniest moments I remember was when one student got hold of almost every toilet roll in the whole hall and unrolled them around a Fry Wing stairwell, festooning it with hundreds of metres of white paper. She got a very very stern telling off from the staff – I don't think they ever forgot what they perceived as an insult.

I made some great friends at CHH, some of whom are still among my closest. But I also hung out with a lot of people who I'm quite glad I've never seen again – people who weren't really like me. I think those years are about really realising who you want to be and who you want to hang out with. But I can't imagine a nicer place to have been while discovering that.

I'm now married to Katie (Durham alumni) with three young boys, we live in Twickenham and I'm editor of *Blue Peter*, the children's programme. I've worked for the BBC for most of the years since I left CHH.

COLIN JACKSON 1991-1993

I remember life in CHH fondly, having arrived as a Fresher and then staying a second year to be President of the JCR. Most of my memories centre around the friends I made at the hall and how genuinely inclusive the whole place felt. In fact, I was only two months into my time at CHH before some of my friends decided to celebrate my birthday by removing the wheels to my car and then sending me on a mission around Hall to find them and bring them back to the bar. Once all the wheels were found, there was just the small matter of getting the wheel nuts back which apparently required that I drink a tequila shot for every nut! Sixteen shots later and there was one lesson from that night... I now know I can never drink tequila again!

Many of the friends I made in those first few months in Halls (even those involved in the 'wheel incident') I am still in contact with now, which goes to show what a lasting effect CHH has had on my life. Mark Jacobs and James Threapleton I still see regularly despite their living in the South East now. In fact, James Threapleton was an usher at my wedding to another CHH alumni – Sally Strong. Sally and I still live in Bristol (in Southville) and we now have two children – Molly and Oliver.

There are many other memories from CHH, from the Sunday night film nights in the JCR to the many Xmas parties and Garden parties which were organised and were such a part of Hall life. I suppose one of the biggest things CHH did for me was to increase my confidence as an individual and help launch me on my chosen career. Since leaving Uni I have worked for the BBC Natural History Unit (one of the reasons I came to Bristol Uni in the first place) and have been lucky enough to be a producer on programmes such as *Springwatch* and *Big Cat Diary*.

I hope CHH is still as vibrant as ever.

Colin Jackson, standing on the right, with James Threapleton (standing) and Mark Jacobs (sitting).

Tim Levell, JCR President, with the Warden at the Christmas Ball in 1988.

Rachel Candlin 1989-1992 and Jeremy Slater 1988-1991
Clifton Hill House provided us with a wonderful start to our university life in Bristol. Its caring, nurturing environment, through the involvement of staff and senior students, provided a sociable atmosphere in which we made lifelong friendships (and marriages!). The dining hall was a great way of meeting people from different disciplines and leisurely daily meals were a delightful way of sharing companionship, whilst away from home. Both of us so enjoyed living at CHH that we wanted to give something back by joining the JCR committee, which is an excellent way of welcoming new students in those nerve-wracking first weeks. Living in the heart of Clifton and in such an elegant building was a real privilege and we remember our days at CHH with a genuine fondness and nostalgia.

Rachel and Jeremy are married with three young daughters. Rachel is a BBC presenter, Jeremy is head teacher at Alcester Grammar School in Warwickshire and teaches chemistry.

Paris Christofides 1992-1999

'Oh it's a laugh here 'innit?'– George the Janitor.

George the Janitor was just one of the wonderful array of characters I got to know during my years at CHH – three as a student and four more as a hall tutor. That catchphrase of his says it all: it was a laugh, from the moment I walked through the hallowed doors as a fresh-faced naïve Cypriot and instantly fell in love with the receptionist (a lovely smiling girl, whose nickname I later found out was actually Smiley), to my moment of departure, turning my back on my second home with stolen cutlery in hand (sorry, Annie). I remember my stay as a colourful succession of moments, events and people – and that's exactly how I'm going to write this, so here goes: my first drunken uni snog in the JCR (to the sounds of 'With or Without You', she wore a red dress and a week later dated my best mate for 8 years): the Gestapo-like stare of Kath Coles, arms folded by the salad bar making sure we didn't pocket an extra bread roll (love you Kath!): the utter chaos of the 'Survivors' breakfast after the Christmas Ball (and the cheats who sneaked off to bed and woke up for it – you know who you are!): Maureen and Margaret, the lovely C floor Fry wing cleaning ladies, barging into my room and waking me up by smacking their brooms all over me: the dreaded fire alarms (it was always burnt toast in South Wing!): forgetting the blasted late door code: the scramble at the pigeon holes on Valentine's Day followed by the disappointed faces at breakfast: that god awful walk up Constitution Hill (shamefully, I flagged cabs at the bottom several times): keeping an eye open at dinner time for seconds (I was very fast, hence why I put on four stone): the wonkey pool table that if you aimed three inches to the left, chances were you'd pot it: accidentally burning a perfect square in the grass of the lawns after using a disposable 99p BBQ (I covered it up with some twigs – sorry, Annie): corridor parties: the walk to the 10 o'clock shop down the road, which shut at 11 – never got that: and finally, smuggling an inflatable plastic sheep called Dolly into the Hall photo (sorry, Annie!).

So thank you CHH for the memories – and thanks to each and every person in it who made it so special. For seven years, you were my second family.

Paris Christofides is a GWR radio presenter.

The 1998 SCR team. Paris Christofides is in the middle of the back row.

JASON WILLIS-LEE 1994-1997

Looking back, it is hard to believe that nearly 15 years have passed since I moved in to Clifton Hill House (or CHH as the Hall was and is universally known) in 1994, my second year at Bristol University where I matriculated to read medicine. At this time, I was still a rather inept and naive young adult with a lot to learn about life, especially the sort of lessons that can really only be learnt outside a university lecture theatre. The previous year I had lived in Hiatt Baker Hall in Stoke Bishop and during that time I quickly learnt that CHH had a reputation as being one of the university's finest halls and not just because it was the catered hall closest to the university. The beautiful architecture and gardens boasted by the hall are unrivalled.

Admittedly, I also thought the Christmas balls, barn dances, and high table formal dinners would be ideal opportunities to mingle with the opposite gender and sure to be a welcome distraction from a demanding university course. My mind was made up. I had to apply.

As I filled in my accommodation form for my second year I made a point to carefully list my extra-curricular activities (mainly musical) and I thought the fact I spoke fairly fluent French might even earn me a brownie point or two with the Hall's French-born warden, Mrs Annie Burnside. The truth is, CHH would simply not be CHH without the personal touch provided by Annie and her staff who are like extended family during any undergraduate's career. I recall Annie being a pillar of support as I went through a difficult personal time with a very overbearing mother and somebody who could easily be approached for help or advice. This example of exemplary pastoral care is not easily forgotten. The Warden's office was always the Hall's motor, her savoir-faire and skilful guidance the key to the hall's smooth management. Fifteen years on in life, I feel very honoured to have kept in touch with Annie and count her as a personal friend. I am only one of many CHH alumni to be forever in her debt.

An anecdote concerning a student one year senior to me whose behaviour had temporarily run amok sticks out in my mind. A large amount of pink paint had been splashed across the front door of the hall, no doubt the product of an alcohol-fuelled Saturday evening of vandalism. Clearly, this was not the sort of behaviour expected of a CHH undergraduate. Despite his vehemently denying the offence on repeated occasions, Annie slowly wore the suspect down during a Gestapo-like interrogation in the Warden's office, convinced of his guilt by the tell tale speck of pink paint below his eyelash. The perpetrator eventu-

Student vandalism to the main entrance door, June 1994.

ally caved in and owned up which no doubt earned him a thick black mark in his university file at Senate House; surely a textbook example on how to crack down on an unruly Bristol undergraduate.

During my second year at CHH I was extremely fortunate to be considered quiet and studious enough to live in Bishop's House. The top floor flat of the house, the official residence of the Bishop of Bristol, was rented out to students who enjoyed the best of both worlds – a taste of independent living and able to take catered meals in the main hall. Rooms were very spacious and provided all the tranquillity needed to optimise university exam grades. I particularly recall taking full advantage of the music room on the bottom floor as I rehearsed the repertoire for the Bristol University Symphony Orchestra and Chamber Choir. All in all, it was a real privilege to live in a Grade II listed building for a year and truly an unforgettable experience.

In short, CHH taught me the pleasures of living in a thriving intellectual community, respect for others, and provided me with lifelong friendships that I continue to cherish to this day. The very same values I hope to convey to my 17-month old daughter over the months and years to come.

Jason is a translator. He is married to a Spanish architect and lives in Madrid with his family.

ROSEANNA CROSS 1996-1999

I guess one of the highlights of each year was the Christmas Ball, which I seem to remember usually ended with a group walking across the suspension bridge to see the sun rise the next morning and then adjourning to the York Cafe for a fry-up. One year, some fellow residents attempted to 'trophy' the fairy lights on the bridge, which involved security being called, but I think it was all put down to 'student high jinks' in the end!

The fantastic thing about living in the hall was the constant opportunity to meet other people. There was always company when you needed it, and I spent quite a lot of time lounging around over drinks in my friends' rooms or in the corridors. The queue for the telephone even ended up being a social occasion (the days before mobile phones), as it used to stretch all the way round the corridor sometimes. However, it did get a bit frustrating when you finally got to the front of the queue and were just about to dial the number, and then the phone rang for someone else!

I also enjoyed the CHH music group and played a few duets with Lisa Mears in some concerts. One year, we played a Bartok duet. We couldn't understand the Hungarian musical tempo signs, but assumed that it was probably *Largo*. Amusingly, we were then informed by a member of the audience after the concert that it should have been played as Allegro! Trust the residents of Clifton

Roseanna Cross and Oliver Godwin at the 1997 Christmas Ball.

to know these things!

I was in CHH from October 1996 until June 1999. I studied English (BA Hons), then did an MA in Medieval Studies and a PhD in Medieval Literature, all at Bristol.

I am currently the Head of Undergraduate Admissions at the University of Bristol.

MARTHA GREKOS 1996-1999

Clifton Hill House has always been ideally situated: it is just a ten-minute stroll from the main university buildings on Woodland Road and barely five minutes round the corner from the Student Union. It also has wonderful views down over the docks and across to Cabot Tower. Students have been so privileged to be able to stay in such a beautiful and historic building with extensive gardens and enjoy all the wonderful facilities it boasts. However, for me, what made CHH special was not just its location or its facilities. It was the second-year students who were on the JCR who took pride in being CHH members and had such enthusiasm for making sure all residents enjoyed their stay and the warden who was (and is) the beating

heartbeat of CHH.

I was a member of the JCR Committee in my second year at CHH (Vice-President and Secretary) and I recall the endless long hours we put in to organise plenty of events during Freshers' Week to welcome the Freshers; we ran the hall bar and various competitions; we organised themed formal meals and discos; and of course the unforgettable and extravagant Summer Garden Party and the legendary Snow Ball at Christmas we threw for all the students of the Hall. There was always an opportunity to meet new people and invite friends and family to events. I recall we had garden party themes like 'In the Pink' and 'Ancient Rome/Greece' and the black-tie Snow Ball had themes like 'The Masquerade Ball'. The students had such imagination when it came to costumes and masks! I remember making my own small mask – I still have it to this day!

Outside the JCR committee, other members of hall would organize different sporting teams and competitions; dramatical or musical events; film evenings and even debates. There was always something happening. You could be involved as much or as little as you liked. The Warden also was always there listening to the students' needs and taking a huge interest in events that went on at CHH. Annie constantly kept a good balance between preserving this magnificent listed building and allowing the students to make good use of it. What other hall could you imagine would allow students to stay in Old Clifton and Callander, in the old building, and make use of the lovingly restored library? I still recall the day when my parents saw their Italian furniture fabric in the library! Quite apt for a Grade I listed Palladian villa.

I always found CHH to be a very friendly and fun hall. I found myself living there for all of my three years at Bristol University. I made very good friends and to this day still keep in touch with them and with Annie. I hope that future students who walk through CHH's door feel the warmth I felt, too.

Martha Grekos is a barrister at Berwin Leighton Paisner.

KATE CARTER 1997-1999

If I had known what a special place Clifton Hill House is to live and work in, I wouldn't have chosen it simply on its being the only catered hall in Clifton! I am extremely glad I did choose to spend my first two years of University life there. It was always a vibrant, lively and caring place, where doors were open and students piled into each other's rooms for tea in the afternoon.

The time of the day I remember most fondly was dinner time... after hiking back up the hill from lectures, most of the hall's residents would queue outside the dining hall and catch up on their news; there was never enough time to talk to everyone that you wanted to. It felt very much

Kate Carter (née Elmhurst) with Dave Carter her future husband, at the 1998 Christmas Ball.

like home, with Mrs Burnside and her staff looking after us all so well.

I was privileged enough to be involved in the JCR for both of my years there, and have fantastic memories of dining on top table; of 12-hour Christmas balls and Garden parties; the opening of the Gothic study and being involved in welcoming new students. I did, however, regret adding a 'Guided Tour' to the events in Freshers' week; all the new students dutifully turned up and Tom Latham and I walked all 200 of them round Clifton and up to the University Campus! I'm not sure that the busy Bristol traffic was particularly impressed either...

There were always many varied social events to keep students occupied in the evenings, from the famous Valentine's and Halloween discos to the now very famous Derren Brown, who entertained us with a magic and hypnosis show. The students enjoyed race nights, formal dinners and an extremely memorable 'Full-ish' Monty performance. The beautiful grounds and house lent themselves perfectly to a student production of *Romeo and Juliet* on a lovely summer's evening, and we were treated to *The Boyfriend* which showcased much of our own hall's talent.

There are many things that will always stay with me about hall life, too many to write down, but of course the most important is my wonderful husband that I met in hall in my first year. They were definitely some of the best years of my life, and I still miss Clifton Hill House, ten years on!

CHRISTOPHER WARREN 2000-2004

What can I say about Clifton Hill House that has not already been yelled at top volume along Regent Street and Constitution Hill at dead of night? I came up to Hall in September 2000, and left in July 2004 (when they found I

was planning on staying forever, and insisted I take my degree like everyone else). In those happy, happy four years, Clifton Hill House was – with fine in loco parentis style – mother, father, cook, housekeeper, laundryman, tutor, nursemaid, judge, jury and executioner. In no other Hall of Residence could I have found such a homely and friendly atmosphere, and been welcomed so warmly. The staff, some of whom I came to know well in my time, were all cheerful, helpful and frequent founts of knowledge about other areas of the Hall, and other Halls of the university; the tutors were true friends, dependable, resourceful and genuinely concerned for their charges in the event of mishap.

My own experience will pay small testament to their concern. Suffering from recurring depression, I experienced the frequent crises that so many students, away from home and under new pressures and expectations, undergo. Everyone from Annie Burnside, Warden par excellence, through to the kitchen and cleaning staff brilliantly rallied around me and kept me happy, healthy and filled with confidence to continue and succeed in my degree. This alone should earn them all my undying thanks. More than the permanent staff and tutors of CHH, however, the spirit and enterprise of its more temporary residents is also a mark of how well the Hall was suited to its task. An excellent music and dramatic tradition was continued and greatly added to during the time I was in residence as, under a new musical director and team, the CHH Music Group put on hit show after hit show, even premiering new writing and contributing to the fabric of the Hall by procuring (with the generous help of the Friends of CHH) new technical and stage equipment for future shows, events and receptions. Funny, inventive, talented and surprisingly versatile, four years of students

during my time (and many more since) have produced a consistently high standard of musical and dramatic output. What are my main memories of life at CHH? So many now crowd in: summer afternoons spent on the rolling lawns in front of the Old House when, during end-of-term exam season the gardens were permitted for quiet revision; many fine evenings spent in the Georgian reception rooms assisting with the reception of friends and guests before High Table meals; time spent catching up on Hall gossip with one of the cleaners, or discussing events and repercussions in reception… For two years I was fortunate to serve as Secretary of the Hall JCR, which gave me excellent experience of the internal running of the Hall, both from the student and staff point-of-view, and which always lent insight to later discussions over facilities, running of events, and so forth.

Many happy returns, Clifton Hill House, and all success and splendour for the next 100 years!

Christopher Warren and friend in the Clifton Hill House dining room.

ALEX DUNLOP 2001-2002

Where do I begin with CHH? I suppose to put my enjoyment of my time there into context it's important to say that I very nearly didn't even stay in halls during my first year at the University of Bristol. However, I eventually decided that in order to make the most of my university experience, halls had to be done. CHH was my first choice because of its location and the fact that it was catered. Indeed, in those days the extent of my culinary abilities was baked beans and smash potato. Which reminds me of one amusing incident whereby the vast majority of my Gutter co-habitants hadn't ever seen 'Smash' in action, and were mesmerised by the true transformation of dried beige granules into creamy mashed potato. But I digress. I remember the first day I arrived at CHH, the chap who showed me to my room was less than enthusiastic about my allocation of floor. When I asked him what 'G Floor' was like, his response was simply 'Oh, The Gutter. Err..'. However, throughout the year I found my room to be warm and adequate. Except for the time I found a tramp in my room ('I'm here to see Danny' was his excuse for

drinking out of my tap. Needless to say, the only 'Daniel' in the vague vicinity of my room had no tramp-esque acquaintances that he could recall). And then, of – course, there was the time when I returned to G.30 after lectures and dinner, only to discover that the entire contents of my room – even down to the last pen – had been relocated to the communal bathroom as a 'practical joke'!

The lads in The Gutter were a great bunch, and we quickly formed a strong bond and went out socially together. Half of the CHH football team lived in my corridor and, to boost morale, we renamed the team 'Burnside's Boys' as we felt that the name embodied the strong spirit of CHH, undoubtedly inspired by our legendary warden, Annie.

Annie Burnside is the spirit of CHH. When we decided to turn The Gutter into a Santa's Grotto for Christmas, Annie accepted our invitation to 'switch on' the Christmas lights. She also dealt with some of our more boisterous behaviour with good humour, although with Annie we always knew when we were crossing the line. Such as the dumb-waiter experience. Yes we'd had a few drinks, but the temptation to ascend from the bar to the dining hall and back down again in a small metal box usually reserved for crockery was too appealing to resist. As a slight fellow, I and most of my co-rebels had no difficulty. Sadly the same couldn't be said for the coach of Burnside's Boys football team, who got stuck halfway through his adventure. The fire brigade were called, Annie rapped our knuckles and we knew never to do anything so stupid again. Except to walk from Bristol to Cardiff in the middle of the night while a gale was raging across the River Severn, but that story is for another time…

It is a testament to the incredible atmosphere of CHH that many of the friendships I formed during my year there have stood the test of time. After bidding farewell to The

Gutter, I lived with many of my friends from CHH for the remainder of my time at uni and I have never once regretted my decision to relinquish my home comforts during my first year, exchanging them for what I truly believe was one of the best years of my life.

I am honoured to contribute my CHH memories to Annie's book to celebrate the centenary of the hall of residence and feel privileged to have lived in such a fantastic place. Here's to the next 100 years!

NICK BARNETT 2004-2005. MEMORIES FROM THE GUTTER

When I arrived at Clifton Hill House in the autumn of 2004 I was greeted by the friendly JCR who told me gleefully that I was 'in the gutter'. My first impression was that this did not sound particularly appealing, but how wrong I was. Although I only spent a year at Clifton my time at the hall was undoubtedly my most exciting and social year, and has forged relationships that are as strong now as they were when we were all together in hall. Part of Clifton's success in my mind was the strong sense of community, but this was not just a regular community but one with quirks. My earliest memory of hall life was when the whole hall community were gathered for the warden's 'infamous' smoking speech, something she clearly took very seriously but managed to inject humour into, by engaging the 'sinner' in a way a pastor would try to reclaim a member of their flock.

Most of my fondest memories revolve around the gutter, by far the furthest corridor away from the hall's social space (a good five minute walk!). This location offered us unparalleled privacy, and as only the people who lived down there ever ventured anywhere near the corridor we became a very united group. There were two distinct social events that really brought us all together, although

After switching the Christmas lights on. G-Floor corridor, 2001.

chronologically not the first Christmas was certainly one of them. Although none of us spent Christmas in hall, we obtained our own tree, wrapped presents and lavished the length of our corridor with metres of tinsel. When everything was just right we invested in some mince pies, some brandy and invited the Warden down to join us for what ended up a genuinely merry evening of festivities.

The last memory I am keen to share of my time at Clifton is of something particularly close to my heart – CHHHC (try saying that quickly after a few drinks). Clifton Hill House Hockey Club was something that my friends and I set up early in the term, organising a custom-made kit with hall emblem and sponsorship and with most of the players coming from the gutter. Renowned as a team of hockey purists we were beaten on penalties in the final in our year in hall, but not to be deterred we stayed together as a team for four years, losing in the final on penalties on every occasion! The formation of the team generated many famous social events including our rainbow three-legged pub golf, which attracted forty odd people! In fact team members were so dedicated to the task of performing well on the pitch that they took to practising in the corridor, and breaking not one, not two, but three windows, and a plug socket! All of course were genuine accidents but a small price to pay for such a happy and well functioning corridor.

As a last little note I would like to pay my thanks to staff and students of CHH past and present, it was being in the hall and wanting to improve it and be part of it that got me so involved in student life and ended with my becoming a Union sabbatical. I am certain that all those students in the hall right now are having just as much fun as I did.

SUNDAS ALI 2003-2005

My first day at Clifton Hill House, that building on the steep slope, is somewhat indelible. Excited and expectant of new endeavours but also extremely nervous with a fear of leaving behind a lifetime, I placed my cardboard boxes containing a treasure of my comfort, in my new room in Callander House, the women's compartment in the Hall. The Hall Bursar's cat, Charlie, bustled around like a guard. Having checked whether the communicatory channels worked, namely the phone and internet, I waved a teary-eyed goodbye to my parents and although slightly adrift and being mindful of my bearings in my new residence, I queued up for dinner with a crowd of unfamiliar faces, for a meal to begin a new odyssey.

The very next day, as one would expect, the Warden of the Hall invited the new students for a welcome meeting. As we sat in neatly laid out rows, a message conveying a sense of shared values and belonging, an appropriate directive of responsibility towards each other and an encouragement for a plethora of creativity and exuberance – were just some of the items on the menu, not to forget the tasteful ride back into the history of this century-old Hall. With the exit from this gathering, began the next two years of my undergraduate study in this communal household, which soon became a home.

Without digging into the past and delving into the minutiae of my experience at CHH, I fondly commemorate the warmth of its traditions and culture, abundance of vibrancy through music and drama concerts, enticing cuisine day and night, fairy-tale winter and summer balls and facilitation for those sporty ones amongst us, all of which provided a well-balanced atmosphere for the mind and body in my formative years. Moved forward I have, but left behind me is memorable twilight still existent in the gardens, lanes and corridors of the Hall, perhaps never to whither away. Perfectly suitable here, I feel, is the saying of Winston Churchill, 'We shape our buildings, and afterwards our buildings shape us.' Precisely.

NIRANJALI AMERASINGHE 2004-2006

I arrived at Clifton Hill House on a typical fall day; slightly overcast, crisp and cool. It was not the first time I had been to England, but certainly the first time I had travelled from Heathrow to a given destination by myself. The 12-hour flight from Sri Lanka had not been overly taxing, but the long wait for the bus at Heathrow had dramatically affected my mood; would I make it in time for the orientation at CHH, which would take place in five hours, would it be too dark for me to find my way, would there be anyone waiting to direct me to the Hall? These were among many questions that occupied my thoughts while I waited. At long last, a bus came and got all those waiting for Bristol. There, a group of university students gathered the newcomers and got us to our respective Halls.

My first impression of CHH as I walked through the reception doors was a sense of warmth. The interior was cosy and I could vaguely smell the dinner that had been prepared for the Freshers' feast that evening. I had just enough time to put my bags in my room before running down to the JCR for the big orientation meeting. My room (in the Old Clifton wing) was a shared one, small but very cosy, with tall ceilings and a certain 'old mansion' feel to it. I sensed at once that I would like living there.

I cannot begin to describe what it was like for a relatively conservative Sri Lankan girl to get thrown into the insanity that is Freshers' Week. It was not just adjusting to a new country, strange food(!) and entirely new surroundings, but the culture shock of adapting to the British youth that struck me the most. In hindsight it all seems easy, but at the time, I went through the cold fear that hits every international student in the first few days of University life. Perhaps that is why I later ran for International Students' Representative for the JCR and got involved in organizing Hall activities, from Freshers' Week to Snow Ball. And I must point out that CHH was a great place for an international student to spend first year. There was a good mix of people, which allowed one to form friends in various capacities; study mates, social friends, musician friends, sports buddies, and most importantly, other international students! The tutors and staff were always so friendly and helpful. I remember many days when I would stop at the reception and chat with whoever was on duty. Whenever I missed home, I would go and talk to Annie Burnside, our wonderful warden, who truly made CHH feel like a home away from home.

The highlight of my two years at CHH was the music. Perhaps I found the music, but perhaps it also found me. Before I knew it, I was involved in all the various Hall productions, directing the CHH Choir and Secretary of the Music Group. We planned 24 hour play-a-thons, charity concerts, open mike nights and a number of other musical events around Hall. I made some of my best friends at CHH because of a shared passion for music. Anyone will tell you that having a hobby at university is a good thing. But to be part of a Hall that enables you to explore the heights of your abilities in the extra activities that you love is something truly special. I could not have asked for a better place to have spent my first two years of university life.

From a social perspective, the CHH Bar was always a great success, even for those not inclined to consume alcohol. We had numerous theme nights and weekend events that brought lots of students to the bar to socialize; the football table and the pool table were in constant use throughout the night. I remember coming back late one night after a concert and finding students in the JCR playing pool, enjoying a few laughs long after the 'event' itself was over. They would invariably be in a costume of some kind – somehow that was a theme for our year. Everyone got out their costumes! A friend of mine once walked into a career-themed night at the JCR without a costume and promptly ran to his room only to show up ten minutes later in his rock climbing gear, fully adorned with rope and hooks and other paraphernalia that I do not care to recall! Oh, we knew how to have fun.

I had two great years at CHH. It saw me through good

above: Nadie Kahatapitiya.

left: Nira Amerasinghe and Ammi (her mother) at graduation.

times and bad; I made friends and lost friends, rediscovered myself time and again, succeeded in some things and failed in others – what my parents would call growing pains of young adulthood. I cannot look back without acknowledging what a vital role CHH played in shaping who I am today. The experience was unique and I will always cherish it.

NADIE KAHATAPITIYA 2004-2008

It was a bright sunny day when I first arrived at the city of Bristol all the way from Sri Lanka. I am the only child in my family and my mother held on to me closely knowing that she had to leave me in a city miles away from home for many years until I finished my Masters in Electrical and Electronic Engineering. I had a mixed feeling of emotions but what overwhelmed me the most was excitement. There were quaint old buildings and some fancy new buildings that passed by while I was driven to Clifton Hill House with my mother, uncle and aunt.

When the car was parked in front of Clifton Hill House, I didn't actually know what exactly I would experience in this place where after four years of residing, I identified it as my home away from home. I had been contacting the warden of the hall, Annie Burnside. before my arrival so my family members decided to meet her first. The moment I saw her with her bright smile and her very warm welcome, I immediately felt at home. She came to me and gave me a very warm hug and welcomed all of us in her cosy office room. Her words and her kindness made me instantly feel secure. That was the initial taste of hospitality I had of my Hall. Little did I know that when the years passed by, the members of the hall became part of the family I created away from home. I made so many friends with the students and the members of staff. During the course of my stay, there wasn't one day I spent with any sense of insecurity.

When I started my Engineering Degree, I had so many doubts about my chosen career path. The doubts grew to the extent for me to consider giving up university. But the warmth of the people, their love and guidance were all an immense strength for me to keep going. I wanted to let go of all these doubts and enjoy university life and hall life while it lasted. I started to take part in many charity concerts within the hall and hall events as well as many other university activities. At this point of time, I was living my dream of performing in so many places in various languages and in various styles. During the second year of my stay in Clifton Hill House, I was elected as the vice president of the Junior Common Room. It was at this point I got to be more involved in the Hall of Residence and be of service to its students.

As the vice president, I was representing many students to voice their opinions and choices for Hall life. I was involved in organising many Hall events such as the famous Snow Ball, Halloween party, Garden Party, Freshers' Week activities, etc…

For me, the time at university was simply magical. It was

a time that passed by so quickly before I even knew it. But one thing I know for a fact is that this journey would have not been complete if it wasn't for my stay at Clifton Hill House. I will never forget the grandeur of the entrance to Old Clifton and my room OC 17. The place I lived for four years and the amazing music room in which I spent many hours getting lost in the world of music, the beautiful gardens which made my day after long hours of studies and the junior common room where all friends met up to have the best of times.

It has been only eight months since I graduated and left Clifton Hill House but it seems like years to me. I miss everything about life in it. As the university completes 100 years I want to give all my good wishes to it, to all the staff members and to the place I call home in Clifton to have more opportunities and strength to educate and accommodate many more students from near and faraway lands and to truly make a mark in their hearts as it did for me. With all the best wishes to everyone at Clifton Hill House and a very special thank-you for making my stay there truly memorable.

ROBERT HOSKINS 2006-2009

Clifton Hill House saved my life. The things I learned (and had the opportunity to learn) over my three years stay have had more impact on my life than, perhaps, even my degree. The people I met and became friends all affected me profoundly. I went into Clifton Hill House a boy and came out a little more like the man I would hope to be.

My first year in Clifton Hill House went by really quickly! What I remember most were the first few tentative nights, where everybody was getting to know one another (many a late night was had chatting into the small hours in the communal kitchen! Where everyone would try and outdo

The *Fame* band.

each other with tall tales of epic parties and past glories), and the final few weeks when I was running for JCR president! The highlight of the year was when I realised it happened to be my birthday on the same night as the Snow Ball! I'm not sure I lasted the whole night!

I ran for president in my second year. I ran because I felt I could give something back to the hall and really wanted to stay another year. After the initial shock of the daunting responsibility involved I started to really, really enjoy it. The sense of pride you feel when you achieve something with a group of others like this is something very special. I also found myself in a committee full of girls I had never spoken to before (with the exception of our Social Secretary and IT Secretary), whom I was expected to be in charge of. This was worrying as I couldn't have asked for a better bunch of level-headed, and downright scary, and intimidating *women* (not girls). We got along absolutely famously and the rest as we say is history. One in particular has become one of my greatest friends and we still keep in touch.

Our first big event was the Garden Party. The litmus test for all new JCRs and the one that usually defines what their term in power will be like... Fortunately I can't remember how it went other than we did ok. Apart from forgetting to put enough bins out. Oh, and losing a hired walkie-talkie in a fridge. For three days.

Time passed and we survived the perils of 'Moving in Day', an eighteen-hour nightmare of moving students into hall (with huge bags) and micro managing the world's smallest car park, introducing ourselves to everyone at the warden's meeting of the first week, to the perils (and very late nights) of managing and being responsible for the dreaded Fresher's Fortnight (I'd never been the last person to leave a club before), until finally we hit the time for the big one. The Snow Ball. The biggest event in the Clifton Hill House calendar.

Deciding on a theme for the Snow Ball is always a tough challenge, reading the previous committees minutes on the matter showed that straight away. The unwritten rule being that you can never under any circumstances repeat yourselves, even if that means coming up with some seriously whacky ideas. The problem with ideas is that they are not always achievable; we had everything from Beach Parties to Gothic/Halloween/Murder Mystery to Cirque Du Soleil themed evenings before we came up with the sensible, perfectly reasonable idea, and never before attempted idea to recreate the Oscars *student style* on a budget that most Hollywood stars would think was a nice lunch out. We even wanted the red carpet, photographer and all.

So we went for it, an indoor red carpet plus photographer leading to a full three-course meal followed by an awards ceremony (complete with PowerPoint presentation!) with categories chosen wisely by the committee (we had some seriously suspect offerings for award titles from everybody) and voted for by the students (who submitted their friends for the awards during the previous weeks). All of this topped off by some ballroom dancing (my own special addition since I hated club raving and wanted to inflict my tastes on everyone else) which went down spectacularly well considering everyone there spent their weekends going deaf down the local clubs! (It's always surprising but students really do enjoy a bit of class.) After this we had the University Big Band and a student band called Blues Peter get everyone excited on the dance floor before finishing in typical student style with a loud, earth shattering and neighbour fury-inducing rave. We also had a casino (with pretend money), photographer, Santa's grotto (with a rather naughty 'Santa' (*cough* Tutor *cough*)) to distract an increasingly merry crowd. What's never quite mentioned is that during all of this the committee aren't meant to be joining in, they are running the show keeping everyone happy (especially security) and staying up till unhealthy hours cleaning up the mess. *Especially the mess.* In the excitement of preparing for the ball we had forgotten a crucial element. *Extra bins.* For some reason we decided to give everyone free ice cream towards the end of the evening. This was a very, very bad idea (especially since by then the two bins in the whole room had overflowed). Ice cream after four or five hours of use gets very thick and (this is particularly important) sticky. It gets into cracks in the floor, seeps into paint work and strips varnish off floors. It is also very difficult to get off suits and dresses. In other words it is a slightly tipsy and very tired JCR committee member's worse possible nightmare. *Especially* at five in the morning.

It looks from the above paragraph that nothing went wrong. This is a lie and when it did go wrong it threatened to topple the whole evening. We had some security issues with a student who decided it would be funny to spray people's suits silver. Needless to say he got kicked out, crept back in and got kicked out again. I suppose the only thing that was funny was that I found him in the street with his pants round his ankles just seconds after he had mooned security.

Also notice how I haven't mentioned that certain committee members forgot to remember to keep themselves sober during the event in case of an emergency? My vice-president felt so stressed she drank a whole bottle of bubbly herself during the meal and had an argument with security about the above hooligan being thrown out. The sight of a five-foot nothing northern lass in heels and a cocktail dress terrifying the life out of a six-foot something security guard has never left me. I was so stressed that I swear I didn't feel at all tired or drunk until I had to clean up ice cream. Others felt so stressed they decided to… *party* instead. It was also this night that I realised that two members of the committee were in fact going out (and had been for a while!). No wonder they always wanted to do JCR assignments together! When all was said and done we had lost only £582. Which compared to the previous years loss of £3,500 was nothing short of a miracle. I also think we had a better time.

By the end of my (very short) term as JCR president we had almost broke even enough times to just have enough money to shell out and buy a really nice *loud* PA system for the JCR and leave the next committee in a good position for the next year. I am still very proud of that. The warden said we were one of the best committees she had ever had and I think we all felt it had been a very good year.

My final year was spent behind the bar in CHH. While we were handing over the reins to a new group of young hopefuls I was busy learning how to manage a student bar. What an education. There I learnt some more valuable managing skills (yet more cleaning skills) and something more important than all those… how to make a good

The JCR, 2006-7:
left to right, back row: David Peek (IT & Publicity Officer), James Furlong (Bar manager), Dipika Aggarwal (Secretary)
middle row: Lisa Smith (Amenities & Sports officer), Atul Dhupelia (Social Secretary), Cynthia Lee (International Students Rep)
front row: Katie Thorpe (Vice President), Robert Hoskins (President), Miranthi Huwae (Treasurer).

cocktail. If I thought running the Snow Ball was difficult managing the (incredibly small) student bar when it is surrounded by two hundred and fifty merry students is something altogether different.

Final year exams came and went and before I knew it I was saying goodbye to what I had come to know as my second home. I had learnt a lot about all sorts of things I had

Copacabana, the 2007 musical from CHH Performing Arts Society.

never dreamed I would (like sticky ice cream, cleaning, and the importance of an extra bin or two). Where the support staff had become family and every nook and cranny was rich with memories. I'd made some lifelong friends both of staff and students and I had also felt like I had earned my place in Clifton Hill House, not just paid for it.

We never realise the value of something like Clifton Hill House until we leave it (often for good) and I can't explain enough the importance and need for a community such as is is is there. Even if only for the first year (and I am the exception to the rule by remaining for three) staying in a hall of residence is an absolutely essential step for students. Away from home for the first time in this friendly environment they can begin to explore and understand who they are and where their real interests lie under the wonderful care of a truly exceptional group of pastoral staff. For me this was crucial and I hope that the tradition of pastoral care and community spirit continues for as

long as the University of Bristol and especially Clifton Hill House stand.

I'd like to finish by saying thank to all the students and staff who made my stay and Clifton Hill House a wonderful and truly unforgettable experience; the JCR committee, Katie, Miranthi, Lisa, Dipika, David, Atul, Cynthia, Joe, Zoe, and Julien; the wonderful staff, Annie, Lynn, Kath, Catherine, Bridget, Fiona, Ken, Alan, all the tutors, kitchen staff, cleaners, and reception staff. To you all from the very bottom of my heart, thank you.

JULIEN CRAMPES 2006-2007

My time at Clifton Hill House has been a major part of my student experience at the University of Bristol. Living in a hall of residence during the first year at University was an excellent way of being introduced to student life. In particular, being part of a close community and developing long-term friendships with students from all continents and with very varied backgrounds was very enriching. Compared to other halls of residence, Clifton Hill House had the added value of being close to the University precinct and the Clifton/Triangle area and of providing good quality catering, which is always appreciated after having to walk back from the library under the usual Bristol rain in the evenings!

Above all, Clifton Hill House is much more than just a hall of residence where first year students eat and sleep. 'CHH' is also about student involvement, development and entertainment through a multitude of activities organised by the students themselves. I was one of many that joined the hall's Performing Arts Society that puts on an average of one show per term involving about 50 students in the casts, bands, technical teams and even production teams – not to mention regular charity concerts and choirs.

Within Clifton Hill House's Performing Arts Society I was given the opportunity to stage manage a musical (*The Boyfriend*), be a front of house manager for the next one (*My Fair Lady*) and even co-direct the first musical of the next year (*Copacabana*). Such experiences helped me develop communication, leadership and organisational skills as well as boost my confidence and creativity in a very supportive environment. Indeed, Clifton Hill House staff and in particular its Warden (Mrs Annie Burnside) were very keen to promote such initiatives and always did their best to accommodate student activities both in terms of space and resources.

Clifton Hill House is also home to a very active Junior Common Room, excellently presided by Mr Robert Hoskins during my time in the Hall. The JCR organised high quality events: Freshers Week, the winter Snow Ball, the springtime Garden Party and six formal dinners – to only mention the major ones – and these events too were encouraged by the hall staff. I was lucky to get involved in the 'JCR' as First Year Representative, participating in the organisation of events and editing the memorable Year-book sold to most residents at the end of the year.

Finally, CHH included many sports teams (football, rugby, basketball, netball, badminton, the infamous 'bin bowling' etc) and its own squash courts and tennis court. Some of these teams even went on to form proper clubs (ie: Clifton Stallions) after the end of our first year in Bristol. I will definitely remember my time at Clifton Hill House as being an excellent experience and great start to my years at University.

KATIE THORPE 2005-2008

I arrived at Clifton Hill House at 7.30 in the morning on the 1 October 2005 after travelling in the early hours from deepest, darkest Yorkshire with my Dad, the dog and a car jammed full of stuff I would never use. As I walked through the archway of the main entrance I was over-flowing with all the feelings one is engulfed with on arrival at University. I particularly remember being just a little bit nervous, but as soon as I entered the building I was met with a very warm welcome and instantly felt that I belonged there.

I don't really remember much of my first couple of weeks as they were a blur of making friends, registration, trying to find my way to Vet School and back without getting lost and exploring the first city I have ever lived in!

During my first year I participated in many Hall events such as playing guitar in the band for the musical *Fame* and working behind the stage during productions. It was through this involvement around the Hall that I was nominated for the position of vice-president on the JCR for the 2006-7 year. On top of my JCR role in my second year I also co-directed *The Boyfriend*. This was my first taste of directing so was a very steep learning curve but one I thoroughly enjoyed and I was particularly proud of managing to persuade a family friend to lend us some fantastic costumes that were used in the West End version of the musical. It was great fun to work with some extremely talented people even though at some points I could have strangled a few of the leading cast members, most notably my lead man who was still slightly intoxicated from the cast and crew party the night before which resulted in a memorable but very successful matinee performance!

The other highlight of my second year was organising the Snow Ball 'A Night at the Oscars' which was another great success. A team of willing volunteers helped the JCR committee to decorate the entire building from floor to ceiling, turning it into a magical winter wonderland. By the time the students started to arrive in their ball dresses and tuxes I felt I hadn't stopped for days but I quickly transformed myself into a lady and then set about enjoying the evening, while keeping a close eye on the proceedings to make sure it all went smoothly, of course. We started the evening in a very civilised manner with a dinner dance followed by the Oscar awards ceremony, with Oscars awarded to people who had shone during the year through their achievements or as 'unique personalities' which brightened up Hall life for everyone. The ball continued through to the following morning when it ended it with the Survivors' breakfast and photograph with most of us looking very slightly worse for wear. I finished the ball sitting in the television room watching the 7am news before going to bed for a couple of hours sleep and then I remember making my way down to the reception to ask where they wanted the decorations taking down first and getting sent back to bed as there was not a single other student up! It was so silent you could have heard a pin drop! The year finished with the outgoing JCR passing over the torch to the new JCR and helping them with their first function, a garden party to celebrate end of exams, and I will always remember this year as being a very hectic but very, very happy year.

In my third year, the autumn term started with a memory that will stay with me for a long time – on the first night of all the new students arriving, my friends and I were playing a late night game of pool when looking out the window I was sure I saw a male student walking up the corridor absolutely stark naked! My friends did not believe me so we went exploring and sure enough we found a naked fresher (only partly covered with a pillow) on the stairs up to reception. While trying to keep a straight face I asked if he was ok to which he replied that he had locked himself out of his room and needed the spare key. We put him in the JCR and then, after having a giggle a safe distance from the room, went to call security to let him into his room. However just before getting to the phone we saw security enter the building so went to let them know of the situation. Security went with us into the JCR to collect the naked student and then walked with him back into his room. It was one of those moments that you wish you had your camera as the naked fresher was walking down the corridor flanked either side by security men of rugby build. A very memorable evening indeed!

I thoroughly enjoyed my time in Clifton Hill House and the three years that I spent there I will remember for the rest of my life as one of the happiest periods in my life so far. While living there I got to meet and work with some great people and have made some excellent friends of both the staff and the students – friendships I am sure I will keep for a very long time.

Annie Burnside
warden

Matthew Garrett
sub warden

Catherine Filmer
sub warden

David Pettigrew
senior tutor

Lynn Powell
hall bursar and tutor

Dawn Burns
tutor

Dane Comerford
tutor

Andrey Bovykin
tutor

Fiona Chapman
executive assistant

Bridget Coles
accommodation manager

Kathryn Coles
catering manager

Georgina McKibbin
assistant catering manager

Andrew Ferguson
senior chef

Gretta Perkins
receptionist

Lisa Stait
receptionist

Who's who at Clifton Hill House, 2009

Dirk Larsen
receptionist

Dora

Nicky Hobbs
receptionist

Glossary of architectural terms

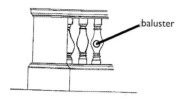

balustrade

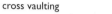

baluster

Architrave: A window or door surround framing a doorway or window aperture

Astylar: With no columns or pilasters

Baluster: One of a series of upright supports in a balustrade

Balustrade: A row of balusters topped with a handrail

Boss: A carved and usually round ornament which covers the intersections of the ribs of vault ceilings

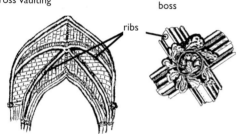

cross vaulting

boss

ribs

Cantilever: A projecting element without supports. Palladio favoured cantilevered staircases where a section of the steps is embedded in the wall thus bearing the weight without any other support

Cornice: Projecting topmost part of entablature, also used on interior walls directly below the ceiling. Usually made of plaster or wood ornamented with classical motifs such as egg-and-dart and dentils

Egg-and-dart: A classical motif of egg-shape forms separated by darts or anchors. Sometimes considered as a symbol of life (ovolo) and death (dart)

Festoon: Carved garland of fruit or flowers suspended in a curve between two points. It is light and narrow at the points of suspension and thick in the middle of the swag

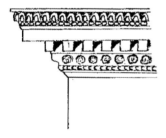

cornice

Finial: Terminal ornament on a post or pediment

Gazebo: An ornamental garden-house usually built at the corner of a garden wall, also called turret or belvedere

Gibbs surround: Decoration of the architrave of a door comprising large and small blocks of stone with a massive keystone and voussoir surmounted by a pediment. Named after Gibbs, the eighteenth-century architect, who frequently used this door surround

egg-and-dart motif

Keystone: The central wedge-shaped stone at the top of a structure. The central stone of the voussoir

Palladian style: The style obeys the classical principles of the sixteenth-century Italian architect Andrea Palladio. The Palladian revival style was introduced to England by the seventeenth-century English architect Inigo Jones. It became widely popular in England in the following century thanks to Lord Burlington, the Whig aristocrat-cum-architect, who presided over the second revival of Palladianism

Pediment: A triangular classical element at the top of a building. Pediments may crown doorways, niches or windows

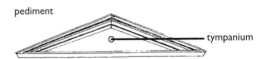

Perron: Platform-landing accessed by symmetrical flights of steps, leading to the 'piano nobile' of a house

Piano nobile: The principal floor of a house, usually the first floor raised above street noise and dirt. It is often of greater height than the storeys above and below

Putto/Putti: Unwinged young male child found in Classical and Baroque painting and sculpture

Rib cross vaulting: A ceiling or roof formed by two vaults intersecting at right angles and ornamented by curved projecting bands (arched ribs)

Rococo: A style that originated from France after the death of Louis XIV in reaction against the heavy classicism of the Sun King. The style is characterised by the use of rock and shell forms, C and S scrolls, curls, foliage, flowers, heads of goddesses, exotic birds and other animals. Isaac Ware described the style as 'A caprice of France'

Rustication: Decorative masonry using heavy stone blocks with deep joints usually reserved for the lower parts of buildings to give an appearance of solidity and strength especially in the case of official buildings or important Italian palaces

Spandrel: Triangular sections above a doorway or on each corner of a ceiling that can be used for decorations and plaster mouldings

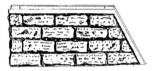

vermiculated rustication

Vitruvian scroll

voussoir

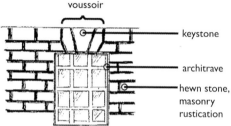

— keystone

— architrave

— hewn stone, masonry rustication

Turret: *see* gazebo

Tympanum: The triangular area within the pediment which is usually ornamented by stone carvings

Vermiculated stonework (rustication): Decoration of stone blocks to give the effect of worm-like tracks, often used for the lower parts of buildings. The roughened texture of the stone suggests solidity and contrasts with the plain ashlar of the upper sections of buildings

Vitruvian scroll: Repeating ornamental scroll pattern, like wave crests, used as a frieze, also called running dog or running scroll. Named after Vitruvius, the Roman architect from the first century BC, author of *De Architectura* who established the three Orders: Doric, Ionic and Corinthian

Voussoir: A wedge-shaped block forming part of the arch of a door or window. The keystone is placed in the middle of the voussoir

Bibliography

Glossary

J.S. Curl, *A Dictionary of Architecture*, 2000

J.H. Parker, *A Concise Glossary of Architectural Terms*, Oxford, 1896

P. Lewis and G. Darley, *Dictionary of Ornament*, 1986

M.M. Pegler, *The Dictionary of Interior Design*, 1966

Chapter I A Palladian Villa

W. Ison, *The Georgian Buildings of Bristol*, Bath, 1978

T. Mowl and B Earnshaw, *An Insular Rococo*, Reaktion Books, London, 1999

T. Mowl, *To Build the Second City*, Redcliffe Press, Bristol, 1991

T. Mowl, 'The Garden at Clifton Hill House', short article, January 1992

T. Mowl, 'Clifton Hill House', University *Nonesuch* magazine, 2002

P. Grosskurth, *The Memoirs of John Addington Symonds*, London, 1984

The Correspondence of Alexander Pope, 1736-1744, edited by George Sherburn, Oxford, 1956

The Letters of John Addington Symonds edited by H. M. Schueller and R. L. Peters, Ontario, 1967

H. Walpole, *Correspondence*, edited by W.S. Lewis, Oxford, 1973

I. Ware, *A Complete Body of Architecture*, 1756

Chapter II Clifton Hill House: its owners and residents since 1750

H.F. Brown, *John Addington Symonds, A Biography*, London 1895, Vol. I, II

Andor Gomme, Michael Jenner, Brian Little, *Bristol, an architectural history*, London, Lund Humphries in association with Bristol & West Building Society 1979

The United Bristol Hospitals, published by the Board of Governors of the UBH, Bristol, 1965

Bristol, Africa and the Eighteenth-Century Slave Trade to America. Vol. II, *Years of Ascendancy 1730-1745*, edited by D. Richardson

The Letters of John Addington Symonds edited by Herbert M. Schueller and Robert L. Peters. Three volumes

P. Grosskurth, *The Memoirs of John Addington Symonds*, London, 1984

K. Furse, *Hearts and Pomegranates, The story of Forty-five Years, 1875 to 1920*, London, 1940

T. Mowl, *To Build the Second City*, Redcliffe Press, Bristol, 1991

J. Pemble, *Venice Rediscovered*, Oxford, 1995

W.T. Pike *Bristol in 1898-1899: Contemporary Biographies*. Two volumes

L. Ponsonby, *Marianne North at Kew Gardens*. Published in collaboration with the Royal Botanic Gardens, Kew, 1990

H. Reid, *A Chronicle of Clifton and Hotwells*, Redcliffe Press, Bristol, 1992, p 80

Miscellanies by John Addington Symonds, M.D., Selected and edited, with an Introductory Memoir, by his son, Bristol, 1871

G. Munro Smith, *A History of the Bristol Royal Infirmary*, Bristol, 1917

M. Symonds (Mrs Vaughan), *Out of the Past*, London, 1925

A Vision of Eden, The Life and Work of Marianne North, published in collaboration with the Royal Botanic Gardens, Kew. HMSO, 1980

Chapter III A University Hall of Residence: 1909 to the present time

E.E. Butcher, *Clifton Hill House, the first phase*, Bristol, 1959

D. Carleton *A University for Bristol, A history in text and pictures*, University of Bristol Press, 1984

Clifton Hill House Old Students' Association, *In Memoriam May C. Staveley, Clifton Hill House, 1909-1934*, Bristol, 1935

K. Furse, *Hearts and Pomegranates, The story of Forty-five Years, 1875 to 1920*, London, 1940

M. Symonds (Mrs Vaughan), *Out of the Past*, London, 1925

Acknowledgements

In the writing of this book, I have been helped by many people to a various degree and I am particularly grateful to Fiona Chapman, Dane Comerford, Sheena Evans, Chris Harries, Nikki Hobbs, Dirk Larsen, Adrienne Mason, Tim Mowl, Mike Pascoe, Peggy Osborn, Gretta Perkins, Lynn Powell, Judy Preston, Anthony Richards, Richard Sanders, Lisa Stait, Mark Steeds, Peggy Stembridge, and Michael Richardson and Hannah Lowery at the Special Collections, University of Bristol. Guidance, advice and encouragement were generously given by Dr John Pemble and Dr Martin Crossley-Evans whose extensive loan of books also helped me enormously.

Personal thanks are owed to the editor, John Sansom for his kindness and professionalism, and to Stephen Morris for his splendid design and photography, for his patience and tolerance of my copious collection of illustrations. Stephen has been able to juggle with our amateur photographs and has added another dimension by skilfully introducing his own artistic and professional touch. I am greatly indebted to Ann Stark who edited all the Clifton Hill House 'Reminiscences' covering the first fifty years of the twentieth century. Ann was a tower of strength in the challenging task of sifting through the archives of the CHHOSA (Clifton Hill House Old Students Association). I am grateful to all the later contributors most of whom were students during my wardenship. I am also indebted to Ann Gray and Anne Martin-Carpenter for their generous donations and the Alumni Foundation of the University of Bristol for the loan and grant which helped towards meeting the printing costs.

I would like to express my boundless gratitude to Gareth Lewis for his careful and patient proof reading and suggestions. His help has been invaluable.

Historical photographs were reproduced with the kind permission of the Special Collections, University of Bristol. Kew Gardens kindly waived copyright fees for the post-cards illustrating Marianne North's work. English Heritage kindly gave permission to use the photographs of the book covers for Chiswick House and Marble Hill. Photographs were taken by Steve Stunt , my two sons, Olivier and Philip, my husband, Marc, and myself.

I should also mention my long-suffering husband, Marc, who put up with my absence from family life during the writing of this book, my son Philip who so willingly put his computer skills at my disposal in organising the many illustrations of the first three chapters and Andy Limmack and Katie Thorpe who assisted so patiently and skilfully for the final two.

Annie Burnside, Bristol, May 2009